Sixties Diesel & Electric Days Remembered VII

Strathwood

British Rail
Electric
Locomotives & Multiple-units
IAN ALLAN
3/-
British Rail
Diesel
IAN ALLAN
abc
BRITISH RAILWAYS
LOCOMOTIVES
& other motive power
COMBINED VOLUME
12/6
IAN ALLAN
IAN ALLAN
a b c British Railways
DIESEL
locomotives
2/6
COMBINED VOLUME
abc
BRITISH RAILWAYS
LOCOMOTIVES
and other motive power
12/6
IAN ALLAN
BRITISH RAILWAYS
DIESEL
LOCOMOTIVES
IAN ALLAN
a b c
2/6
abc
BRITISH RAILWAYS
LOCOMOTIVES
Diesel and Electric Locomotives
2/6

Sixties Diesel & Electric Days Remembered VII

Front Cover: It's June 1962 and 10000 is using all of its 1,600hp to climb Camden bank with a down outer suburban service, even though it was being banked in the rear on this occasion. Six months later and she would be set aside into storage at Derby Works never to work again, her fifteen-year working life over already, but with over 1,000,000 miles of service given. *Colour Rail*

Strathwood

Sixties Diesel & Electric Days Remembered VII

A selection of some of the essential books and magazines from the era along with a few other reminders of the locomotives.

First published 2022

ISBN 978-1-913390-81-5

All rights reserved. No part of this book may be reproduced or transmitted in any form or by any means, electronic or mechanical, including photocopying, recording or by any information storage and retrieval system, without written permission from the Publisher in writing.

Copyright Strathwood 2022

Published by Strathwood Publishing, 4 Shuttleworth Road, Elm Farm Industrial Estate, Bedford, MK41 0EP. Tel 01234 328792
www.strathwood.co.uk

Contents

	Page
Preface	6
Recollections of a Night Hawk	7
Sulzer Sounds	12
Tinsley Walkabout	26
Blue is the Colour	42
Eastern Electrics	57
Under the Wires	73
Two Tone Traction	93
Type 1 Miscellany	113
What's in a Name	134
Works Visits	150

Preface

For this volume, I have asked one of the great spotters from the steam era to give us a taste from some of his memories from the sixties. Unlike so many of the steam era spotters and cameramen, Patrick did not turn his back on the ever-increasing waves of new traction appearing on our railways every month. Instead, he embraced it all as part of the hobby and whilst continuing to chase the last few elusive cops for his Ian Allan ABC, he recorded the numbers of all the new diesels and electrics too.

We will be publishing a full volume of reminiscences from Patrick through the 1950s and 1960s in the future, complete with a wonderful collection of colour images from the era. Patrick's stories are a delightful reflection of our hobby during perhaps its heyday, as the British Railway's steam fleet finally stopped being increased, and the thirst for change and modernization saw an entire way of life swept aside in the following years.

We will all have our favourites from the past, I hope you will enjoy this compilation and we must also thank the foresight of the photographers and the kindness of those who have allowed their work to be seen and appreciated by a wider audience too.

Kevin Derrick
Perth 2022

Below: The new generation of West Coast Main Line power began with English Electric Type 4 1-Co-Co-1s, but they soon morphed into the more powerful Brush Type 4, Class 47s before the Class 50s took control until electrification. In April 1968, D1854 from the LNWL pool heads south at Beckfoot with a service from Glasgow Central to Euston. *David Ford*

Introduction - Recollections of a Night Hawk

Our story begins back in the earlier days of what would be later known as the swinging sixties at a time when new diesels and electrics were replacing ageing and not so old steam locomotives every month. As a result, dedicated spotters sought to more desperate means to pursue our hobby.

Shed bunking visits in the dead of night was a matter of keeping your wits about you, always on the lookout for the foreman's office and the ever-present danger of stepping into red hot ash, or tripping over clutter strewn all around engine sheds along with light engine movements. All of this was carried out with the aid of a simple pencil torch to guide me. After two or three nights dossing on trains feeling ready to drop trying to keep to a tough timetable, it was always a great temptation to cut corners, taking a risk rushing around a shed, dashing over running lines with the prospect of tripping over signal wires or other obstructions laying in wait within the darkness for tired feet.

But as I gained experience shed bashing, my confidence grew on my nocturnal bunking visits, and as the years progressed I had it down to a fine art. However, there was always the odd occasion when I was caught bunking a shed and unable to talk my way out of trouble and was of course thrown out.

One such instance was after a Northern Railfans Club tour of motive power depots in the Sheffield and Lincolnshire areas one Saturday in March 1961, after the coach dropped me off in Sheffield's city centre. I decided to nip over to Doncaster for an evening bunk of the shed.

Likewise on the East Coast Main Line, the English Electric 1Co-Co1s gave way to more powerful Co-Co designs, in this instance Deltic D9015 Tulyar as it heads for Kings Cross in charge of the up Flying Scotsman service running easily through the Newcastle suburbs at Heaton on 28 March 1965. *Chris Davies/Rail Photoprints*

per usual everything went to plan with three quarters of the shed bunked, copping Class A3 60047 Donovan in the process along with Class A1 60122 Curlew and a few new diesels, I made an error in letting my guard down and low and behold I felt a large hand upon my shoulder in the shape of a very excited yard foreman who was not in the mood for any of my weak excuses, as a result I was frog-marched out!

Back on the station and sitting in the buffet I began forming my plan of action, to return and to finish off my bunking session at the shed, come what may I did not want to be beaten. Two hours later returning under the cover of fading light, this time I enjoyed complete success copping another twelve locomotives on shed from the six roads I had missed several hours beforehand. On the way out one of the shed staff even offered me a lift as he was passing the station and told me a fitter had spotted me earlier and tipped off the yard foreman to keep himself sweet. So, I learned a valuable lesson to try and keep clear of all shed staff and treat everyone as though it was my first ever shed bunk, and not to get over confident again.

Catching a late evening train back to Sheffield Victoria to while away several more hours that night before my booked train to St. Pancras early on the Sunday morning, I decided to sample the delights of the new buffet at the Steel City's now long-lost station. It was open until my train was due at 06.00 on Sunday morning which suited me very well as trying to stay awake all night was always tough. For some obscure reason, the buffet over at Sheffield Midland station closed on Saturday night into Sunday morning, yet it was open all night throughout the week. But I didn't dare to doss down in the warm waiting room at Victoria, trying to keep awake platform spotting at both stations during the long night hours instead, having booked my cheap Sunday excursion ticket to St. Pancras for the next stage of my weekend bash to bunk several of the London sheds. Settling down in the waiting room along with several other passengers, I was very lucky to find a spare bench and giving myself up to the arms of Morpheus along with other sleeping forms laying sprawled all around the room.

In the staff room a card school was in full swing on a grubby table lay a pile of coins topped with a ten-shilling note, in another corner a couple of porters were fast asleep in two moth eaten armchairs. The red-faced platform foreman reached out for the cash only to be stopped in his tracks by a grinning shunter, aces high mate its my pot! You're a ruddy cheat, prove it laughed a post office worker, its fair he had the best hand. As a result, the livid foreman turned his fury to the hapless newspaper staff telling them it was about time they moved that pile of News of the Worlds away from the down platform! The vans haven't arrived yet was the response, I don't damn well care, get them off the platform NOW! He then turned towards a porter reading a torn page of a Sporting Life, never mind those ruddy horses wake those sleeping beauties over there, we've got the Glasgow running in, and don't forget to check the van at the back.

Just before 04.00 the Glasgow to St. Pancras via Derby arrived and I was now alone in the waiting room pressing the wall heater switch falling

Destined to be exceedingly rare north of here during their short life span, one of the last built Clayton Type 1s, D8612 arrives light engine at Perth on 18 July 1966. In fact, this example only managed to put in less than six-years' service until withdrawn in October 1971, then it was dumped in Glasgow thereafter for almost four years before scrapping. *Bill Wright*

towards a deep sleep, waking with a start to the rumble of a lengthy line of barrows full of mail and Sunday newspapers being pulled by a station tractor driven by a half-asleep porter hunched in his greatcoat. Then the sleepy voice of the station announcer echoed around the deserted platforms "Nottingham Midland, Kettering, Luton Midland Road, and London St. Pancras – the 10.05pm train from Edinburgh Waverley now approaching". A shiver of excitement ran through me as it never failed to do and I was back in my element from the long night hours, suddenly out of a mirky night the low whine of a reasonably new Peak diesel rumbled into sight, pulling its long train into the platform, I'd expected a Jubilee, but my disappointment back then didn't dampen my anticipation for the journey ahead.

The platform lighting shone down through the hoar frost, and the tired eyes of the locomotive crew were quite surprised to see a lone passenger waiting. It was just before 05.00 when the train came to a halt with steam heating sizzling between each of its coaches from the Peak's efficient boiler. To my delight I found plenty of room onboard with just the odd compartment in darkness with a sleeping form to be vaguely made out. The previous departure from Glasgow St. Enoch likewise bound for St. Pancras just an hour beforehand was quite full, so my luck was in, diving into an empty compartment in the front Second Corridor coach next to the Brake Gangway coach and the locomotive. Quickly pulling down the blinds and switching the roof lights onto dim, before kicking my shoes off and folding my donkey jacket into a pillow. Having pushed the armrest up I was able to stretch out on the stale smelling seats, dead to the world just as Peak D11 opened up pulling away once more leaving the deserted platforms piled high with mail and Sunday's newspapers. The carriage bogies of the Anglo-Scottish night express then clattered over the point work leaving a grim city to wake from its slumber to yet another grey dawn over the tower blocks.

On one seven day shed bash using a London Midland rail rover in September 1963, travelling on night trains getting very little sleep during the first half of the week, it was tough work having to stay awake to change trains in the early hours enroute to visiting MPDs in North West Lancashire. With just one night's kip dossing on the 11.55pm Manchester Piccadilly to Euston service which due to permanent way work for the impending electrification south of Crewe was to be routed via the Great Central main line instead. I found myself waking only once for the call of nature and peering under the compartment window blind in the early hours at Nottingham Victoria to see what about, we arrived an hour late at Marylebone. However, I wasn't complaining as I gained an extra hours of sleep and I was now no longer forced to hang around waiting for the tube to open at 05.30. Later that week upon reaching Carlisle just after 10.30pm on a Saturday night heading for the 'night buffet' with just over twenty-five hours left on my rail rover. My intended

On duty today with a Bristol to Newcastle service showing the headcode 1N24 in its split headcode boxes was D30 from 55A Leeds Holbeck shed as it passes York's then diesel depot coded 50A on 6 October 1968 and heads northwards. *Chris Davies/Rail Photoprints*

itinerary for the Sunday was set to include depots in Sheffield, Buxton, Stockport, Stoke and Stafford, it all looked good on paper at least! But I hadn't realised just how tired I really was…

The 12.44am train to Sheffield Midland (the 10.05pm ex Edinburgh Waverley to St. Pancras) would be handy for an early start at 04.30am bunking the Sheffield depots, which was the plan anyway! It would bring a bonus of a good doss down via the Settle & Carlisle route, from memory I had enjoyed this service south of Sheffield two years previously and would have a good chance of getting a compartment to myself. Trying to keep awake was a major effort, but I didn't dare go into the railway staff canteen for a hot meal in a warm room for fear of dropping off. So, it was a case of walking the cold platform for the next hour or two.

Aside from the odd freight and light engine movement things were noticeably quiet as you expect before midnight until the next flight of overnight expresses for the south passed through. The 11.56pm arrival from Glasgow St. Enoch departed on time for St. Pancras quite well loaded, followed by the 12.08am service for Kensington Olympia which in common with several Anglo-Scottish overnight expresses were diverted from their normal destination which would be Euston as was my own train from Manchester a few days previously.

With the platforms now empty of travellers and the clock showing 12.35am, at last out of the mist-shrouded night came my train hauled by the now usual Peak diesel. To my joy it was very lightly loaded leaving the whole front coach to myself. My chosen compartment was both clean and warm, after dimming the lights and my usual routine pulling the blinds down etc I fell into a deep sleep. Some time later the carriage wheels were silent and the usual sound of roaring steel wheels upon rails was missing, in fact the train was at a standstill. Lifting the blind trying to focus my now bloodshot eyes, they fell upon the station sign. To my horror it read Nottingham Midland, oh hell I've overslept and for the briefest of moments I was tempted to go back to sleep in my nice warm cosy compartment. But, as luck would have it the locomotive was running round its train giving me just enough time to gather my thoughts and my belongings, diving out of the nearest door onto a cold platform at what turned out to be 05.50am. There was nothing for it but to back track cutting out the Sheffield area sheds, and to head for Bury via Manchester and Skipton the long way around. One bit of good fortune was that my next service was at 06.45am to Derby, not so long to wait at that time on a Sunday morning, things could have been an awful lot worse... I could still always visit the other MPDs on my hit list that were missed out at a later date with the Northern Railfans Club arranged coach tours.

After copping my last steam locomotive in April 1964, I decided to carry on and to try and complete all the diesel and electric locomotives still required for my collection, plus booking the much-maligned DMUs and EMUs just to help fill the pages of my notebook, thereby giving me the perfect excuse to continue travelling on what was by now mostly diesel hauled overnight expresses. Looking back now I can recall many fond memories from those years ago around our great hobby, how about you?

Patrick Evans
Sanday, Orkney

Opposite: A perhaps less glamorous duty maybe but nonetheless a once valuable source of income to the railways was the transfer of iron ore around the country. Here at Belvoir Junction on the Nottingham to Grantham route, D8122 and D8187 shuffle about light engine between just such duties during September 1968. *David Ford*

While others were out chasing the last remnants of steam in the North West, thankfully some cameramen still chose to record diesel scenes such as this near Harrogate during April 1968, as D1573 from 52A Gateshead heads a short up parcels service. *David Ford*

Sulzer Sounds

Fitting perhaps to begin at Derby during 1968, a full decade after the first examples of what would become a large fleet of Sulzer powered locomotives left the workshops to the right in July 1958, with the release of D5000. In the meantime, Derby had seen many changes in the locomotives seen in the city every day. But one continued factor began to dominate in the sounds of Sulzer powered Type 2s and Type 4s which would remain constant into the 1980s. Further signs of the times as D108 departs past one of the then many former Midland Railway signal boxes controlling the route amidst the ever-increasing numbers of blue and grey coaches. This next view at York taken during June the same year portrays the stabling point among another potential cacophony of Sulzer clatter. Centre stage D1105 was just twenty-months old at this point, although released from Crewe Works in November 1966 in two-tone green she was originally adorned with a small yellow warning panel. A recent visit back to Crewe has seen her up-dated as is one of the Type 2s in the background beyond what would be your author's very last Peak, D138. *Photos: Strathwood Library Collection & Colour Rail*

Taken while the Northampton to Bedford branch was being dismantled as demolition trains were being run several times a week. One of these was captured at Hardingstone Crossing near Northampton. Previously this section of track had been shared by the Wellingborough and Bedford lines once St. John's Street station had closed. On this day D5059 along with sister D5057 following light engine were both in action. The date was a rather wet and miserable 10 April 1967. A visit the same year to Toton on a Sunday to maximize the locomotive numbers to be seen, found the former steam shed's coaling plant still standing sentinel over D5 Cross Fell sandwiched in between fellow Class 44s D1 Scafell Pike and D7 Ingleborough.
Photos: John Evans & Dave Langham Collection

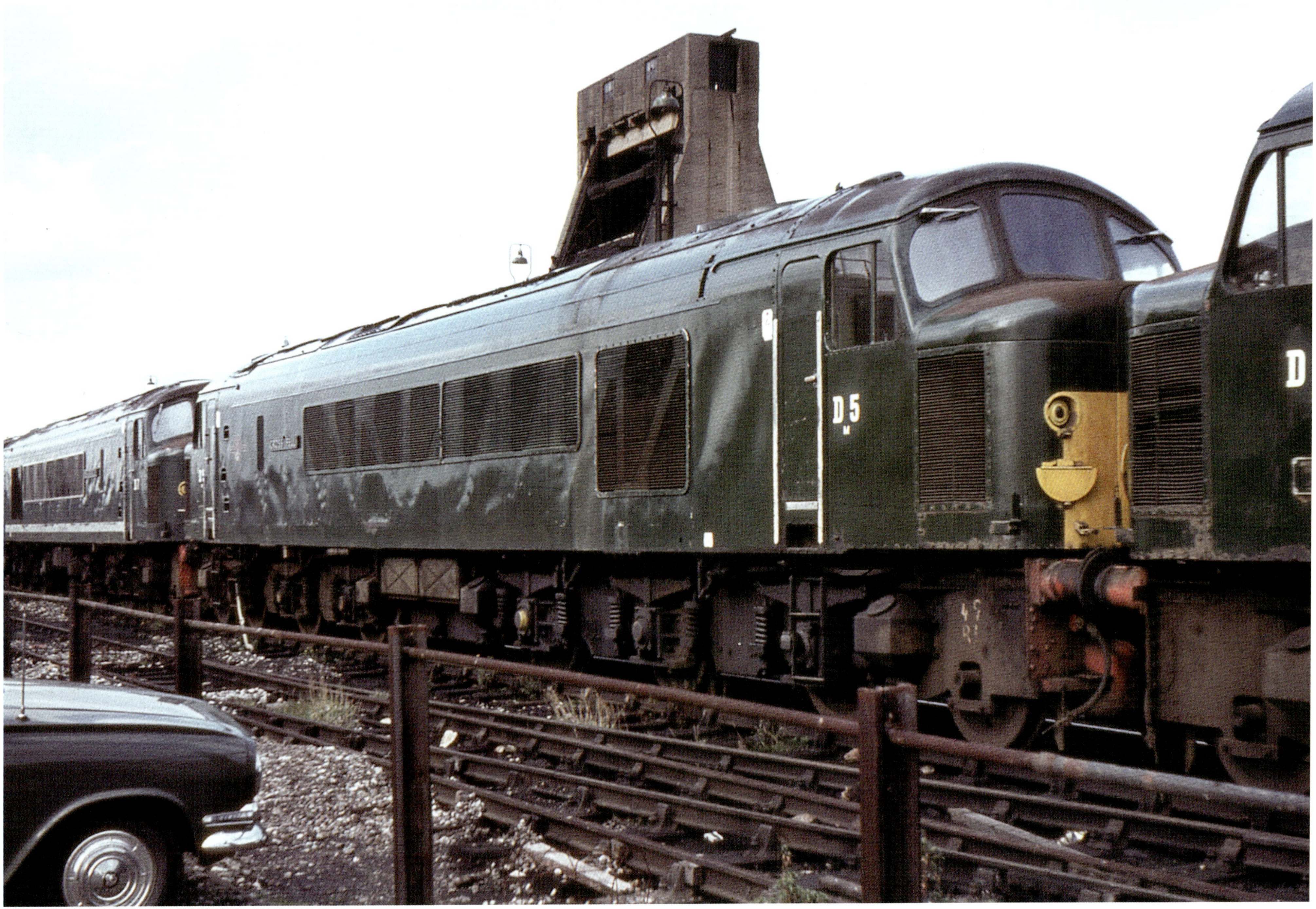
D5

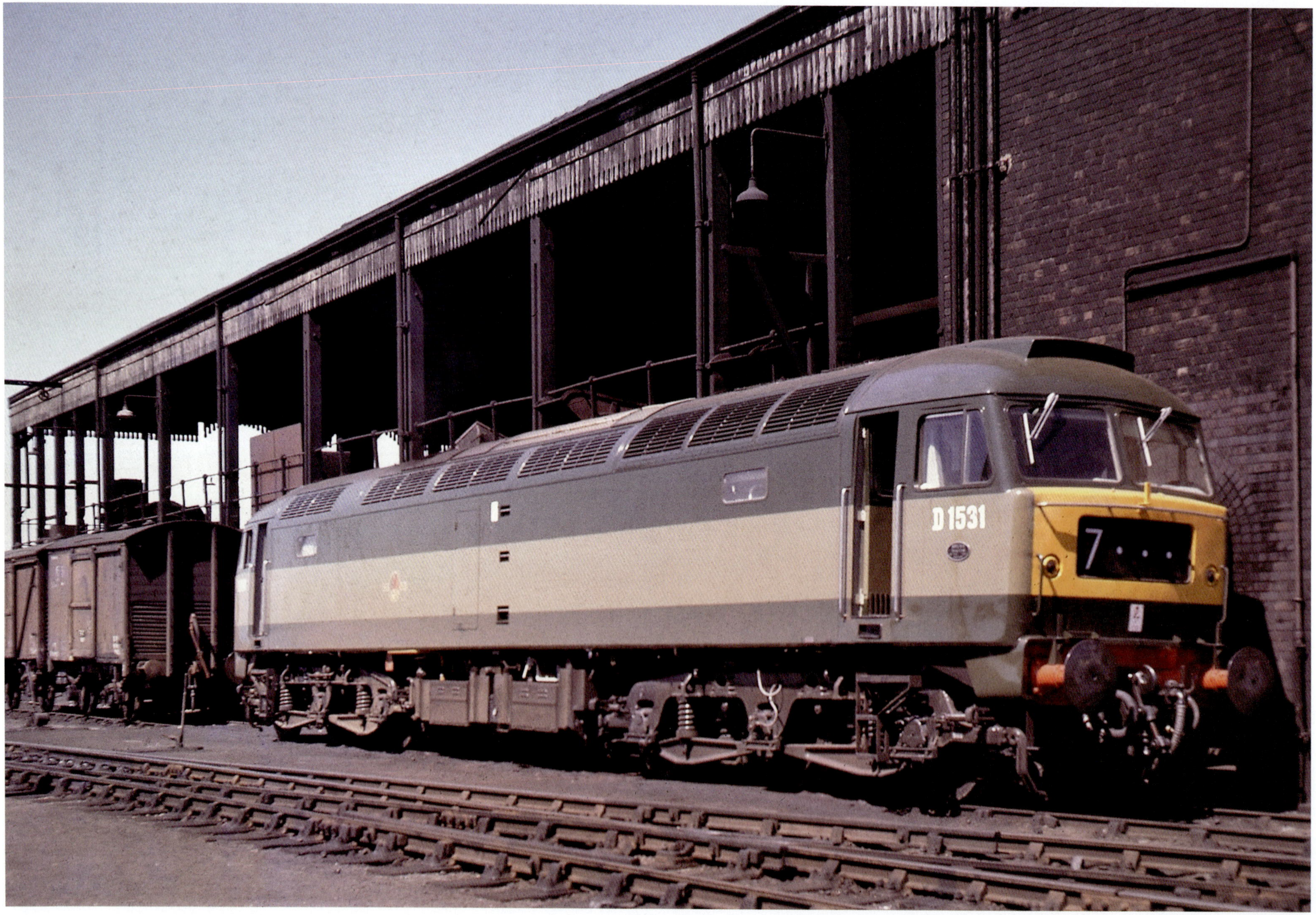
D 1531

Opposite: A modest layer of soot has already built up on the paintwork of the freshly delivered D1531, stabled here alongside the more primitive coaler at New England just a few weeks after this Brush Type 4 had been put into traffic on 15 July 1963 and allocated to 34G Finsbury Park. New England shed closed to steam on 27 February 1965. *Rail Online*

The driver of D150 will be doing his best to control the speed of his seven-month-old Peak from 17A Derby, dropping down the sharp incline from the Lickey Hills into Bromsgrove station on 23 July 1962. From the arm hanging from the window, we might assume his secondman is riding in the rear cab for some reason. *Colour Rail*

A much more generous coating of diesel and steam soot adorns the roof of D5123, as one of 60A Inverness depot's long-term Type 2 residents when seen light engine at Perth on 17 July 1965. Standard fittings for Highlands based locomotives often included snow ploughs fitted all year and the conveniently positioned tablet catcher below the driver's window at this number 2 end. *Colour Rail*

Opposite: The number 1 end of D5267 shows signs of how the corrosive elements within the locomotive's coolant system could affect the paintwork if unchecked, as this modified later batch Type 2 stands alongside a duo of Class 44 Peaks in the yard at Toton on 16 February 1969. Visitors to the massive depot here on a Sunday could be well served with a large number of entries into their notebooks. *TOPticl*

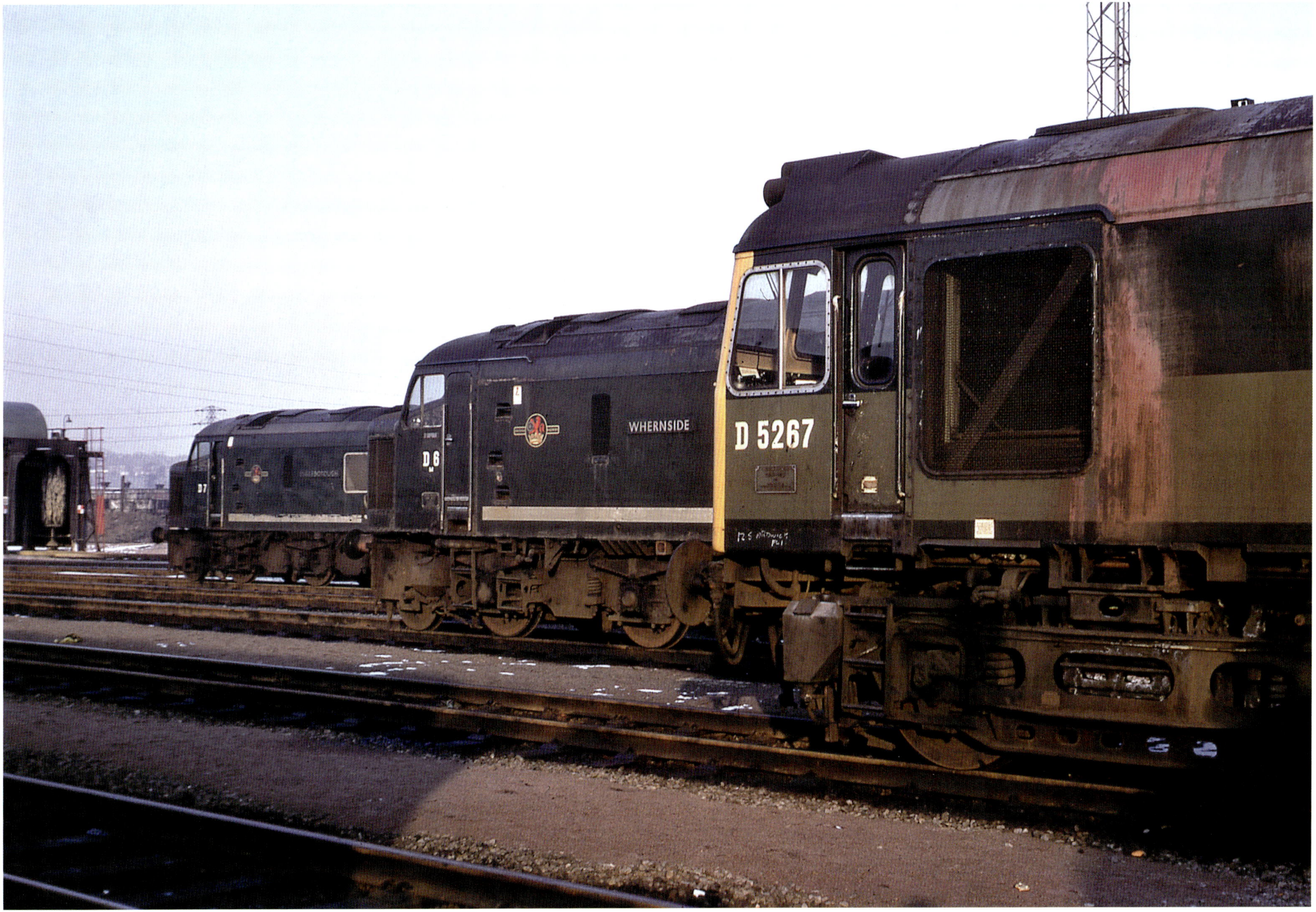
WHERNSIDE
D 5267

20

Opposite: Just imagine for a moment the clatter of their distinctive Sulzer exhaust echoing back from these three early build BRCW Class 26 locomotives congregating around Blackford Hill signal box in the Edinburgh suburbs on 28 May 1968. All three would be allocated to 64B Haymarket but often to be found also out stationed at the depot established at Millerhill too. We do not have the identities of the two examples on the left as Class 26/0, but the one signaled away with the Blue Circle Cement presflo wagons is a later Class 26/1. *Colour Rail*

It is a fitted freight duty today for D1587 from the 81A Old Oak Common allocation as they run her through the countryside near Cheltenham in 1965. At this point the Western Region was still applying their route coding spots to their diesel fleet, hence the red spot below the Crewe Works builders' plate on the cabside. The red spot denoted in this instance their axle loading being up to twenty tons, thereby precluding their use on some lighter laid routes. Class 42 and 43 Warships and Class 52 Westerns were likewise coded the same as red spot. *R.C.T.S. Archive*

The preferred provider to the Southern Region for their allocation of a general-purpose Type 3 locomotive was a BRCW design fitted with a Sulzer 1,550hp engine providing a tractive effort of 45,000lb. A visit to 73C Hither Green on 20 April 1969 finds D6584 still retaining her green livery, albeit updated with full yellow ends. Notice how the doors are bearing paintwork scars from footplate crew's giving them a hearty kick very often upon overcoming any stiffness in opening. The appearance of Class 46 Peak D165 at Toton looks clean and tidy as it stands set aside awaiting repairs with its wheels chocked in the company of a likewise lame Class 08 shunter. **Photos: Dave Cobbe Collection/Rail Photoprints & Dave Langham Collection**

23

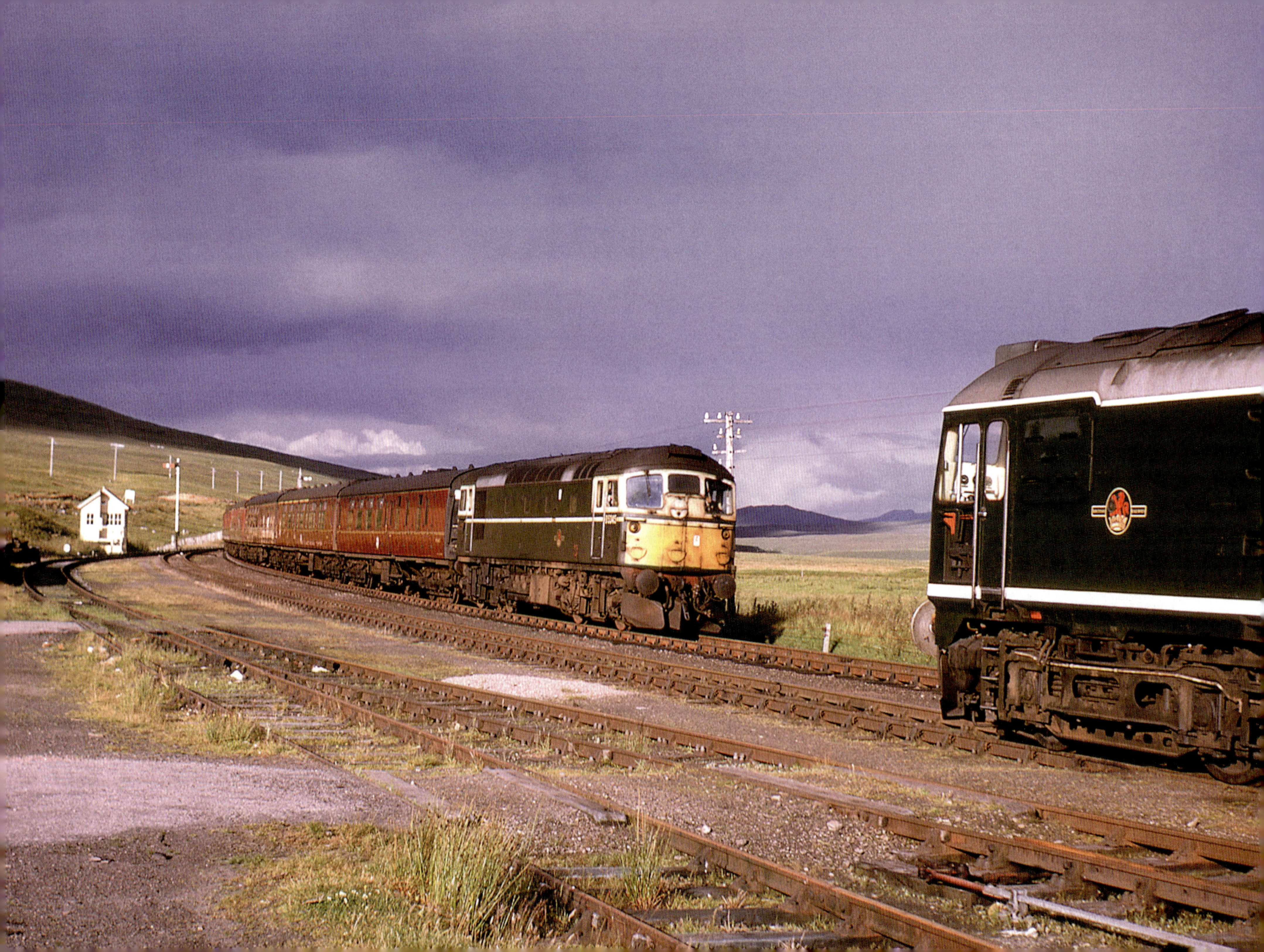

Opposite: A moody looking sky greets the arrival of Class 26 D5345 heading for Kyle of Lochalsh into the remote and lonely station at Achnasheen during August 1967, as one of Inverness depot's Class 24s awaits access to the single line to head back home. *TOPticl*

Another duo of Sulzer Type 2s are seen as a pair of Class 25 hauled coal trains are found at the once busy Lenton Junction near Nottingham in November 1966, with D7560 from the D16 Nottingham Division being given the clear signal. *Colour Rail*

Tinsley Walkabout

A visit to the once sprawling yard and depot facilities to be found at Tinsley in Sheffield was a must for many spotters, especially if they wanted to clear their Class 13 hump shunters. In this view looking down onto the 1,500v dc catenary feeding the freights to and from the Woodhead route, a well-presented D4501 brings a rake of empties past our camera position. The maintenance shed coded 41A was situated at a higher elevation above the yard with a large allocation of locomotives including on this visit this newly allocated D6705 to the Sheffield area at 41C Wath in November 1967.
Both: Dave Langham Collection

Such was the need to service such a large number of visiting locomotives and engine crews a smaller servicing and stabling point was established at a lower level adjoining the expansive marshalling yard. These views show both these two Tinsley allocated locomotives D5843 and D6818 alongside D6752 also once based here but since August 1967 it had been a 32B Ipswich based locomotive, in these views from early in 1968. *Both: Dave Langham Collection*

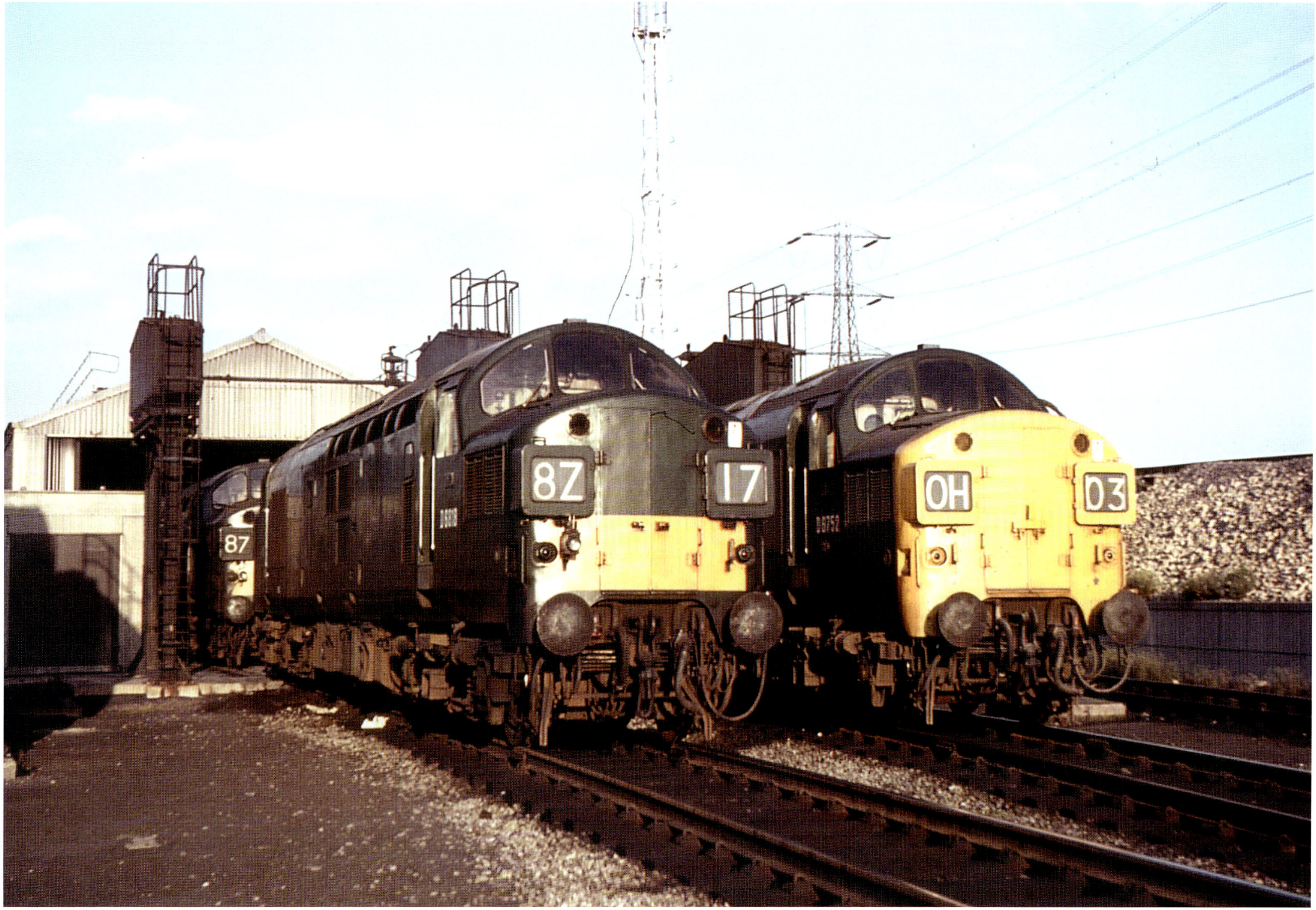
87
8Z
17
OH
03

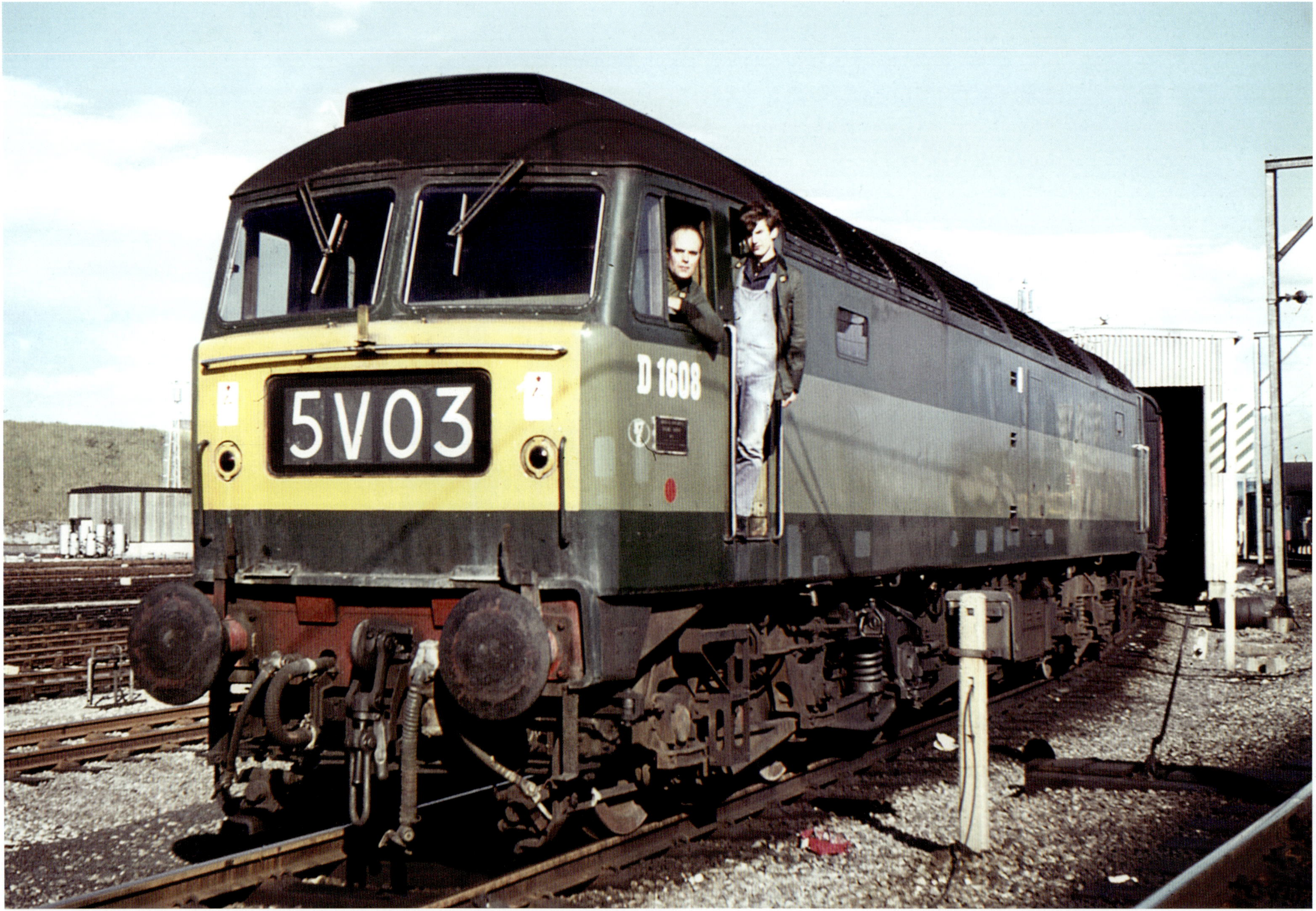
5V03
D 1608

Still showing her 87E stenciled shed coding from her early days when she was new in August 1964, this shot was posed we think, in the servicing point yard during the summer of 1967 when the now patched up D1608 was also in the custody of 82A Bristol Bath Road. Likewise, D5556 still carries her 30A Stratford shed plate underneath the Brush Traction builder's plate and was freshly transferred here to 41A Tinsley in February 1967 as she stands alongside a Class 37 by one of the fueling points at the maintenance depot. *Both: Dave Langham Collection*

A stroll back to the servicing depot adjacent to one of the overhead electrified roads brings us a close-up cab study in the early summer of 1966 with both locomotives at this time being allocated here, although D8128 the first of the headcode box fitted machines was about to be transferred away to nearby 41E Barrow Hill that June. When it came to TOPS renumbering D8128 became 20228 in January 1974 in an attempt to keep the headcode box fitted class members consecutively numbered, as the former D8000 with its disc headcodes assumed the TOPS number as 20050 in February 1974, and D8050 likewise fitted with headcode discs took up the number of 20128 previously in November 1973. Meanwhile D1541 went on to be renumbered as 47429 in February 1974, albeit by then allocated to Gateshead. In January 1987, her withdrawal was announced but her scrapping only followed two years later at Crewe Works by outside contractors A Hampton. The future for D8128 would be more fortunate as she survived on British Rail's books until July 1991, eventually after a spell operating in France she joined the ranks of preserved diesels. Whereas the fate of Tinsley's once proud marshalling yard and depot which was opened in 1965 as part of a major plan to concentrate all of Sheffield's rail freight would be one of slow decline in the decades that followed. The maintenance depot closed on 27 March 1998 and the weed strewn remnants of the yard become increasingly disused in the following eleven years. However, this was the scene back in 1967 as an unknown English Electric Type 3 rolls by with another load of rail borne freight.
Both: Dave Langham Collection

32

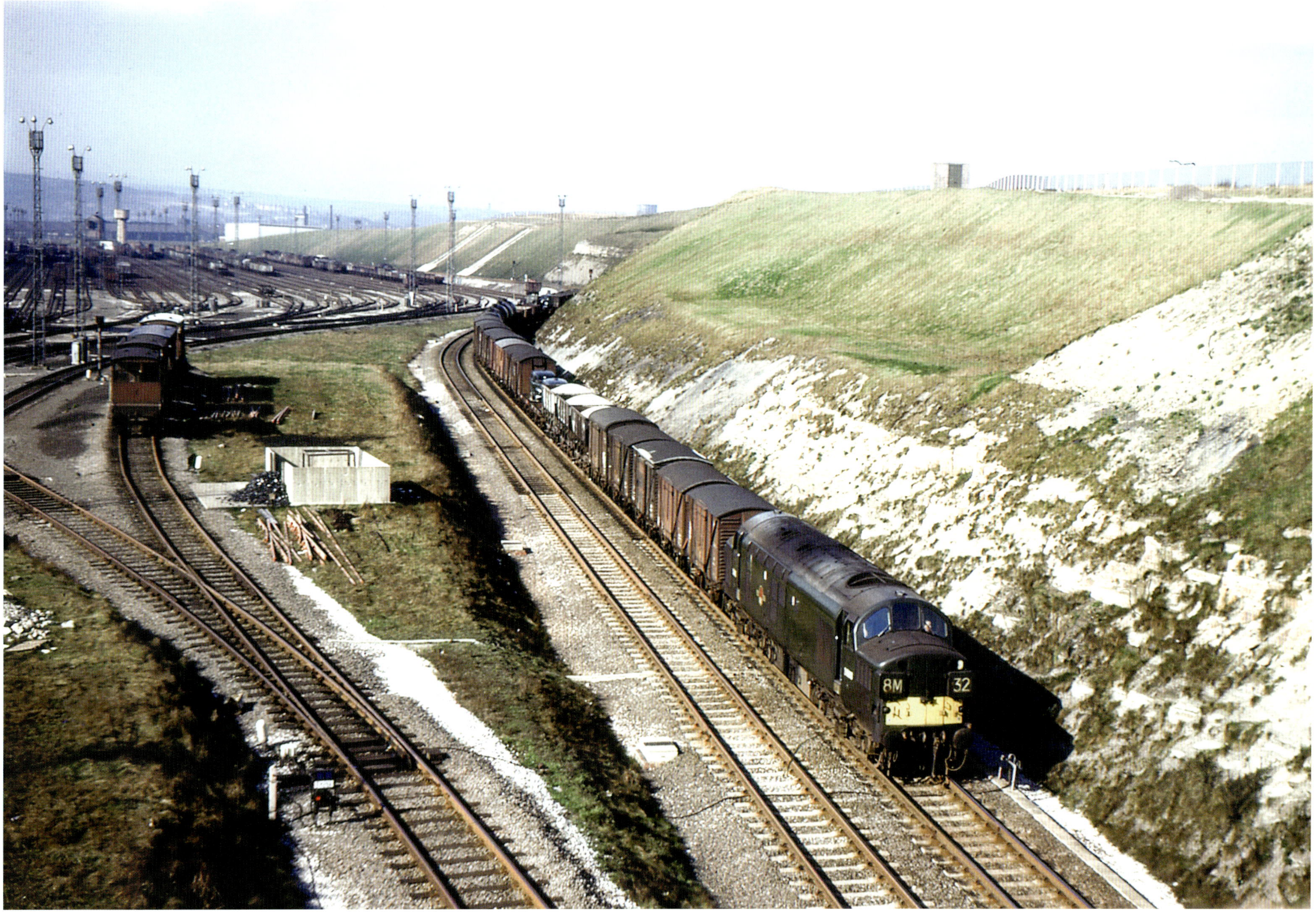
8M
32

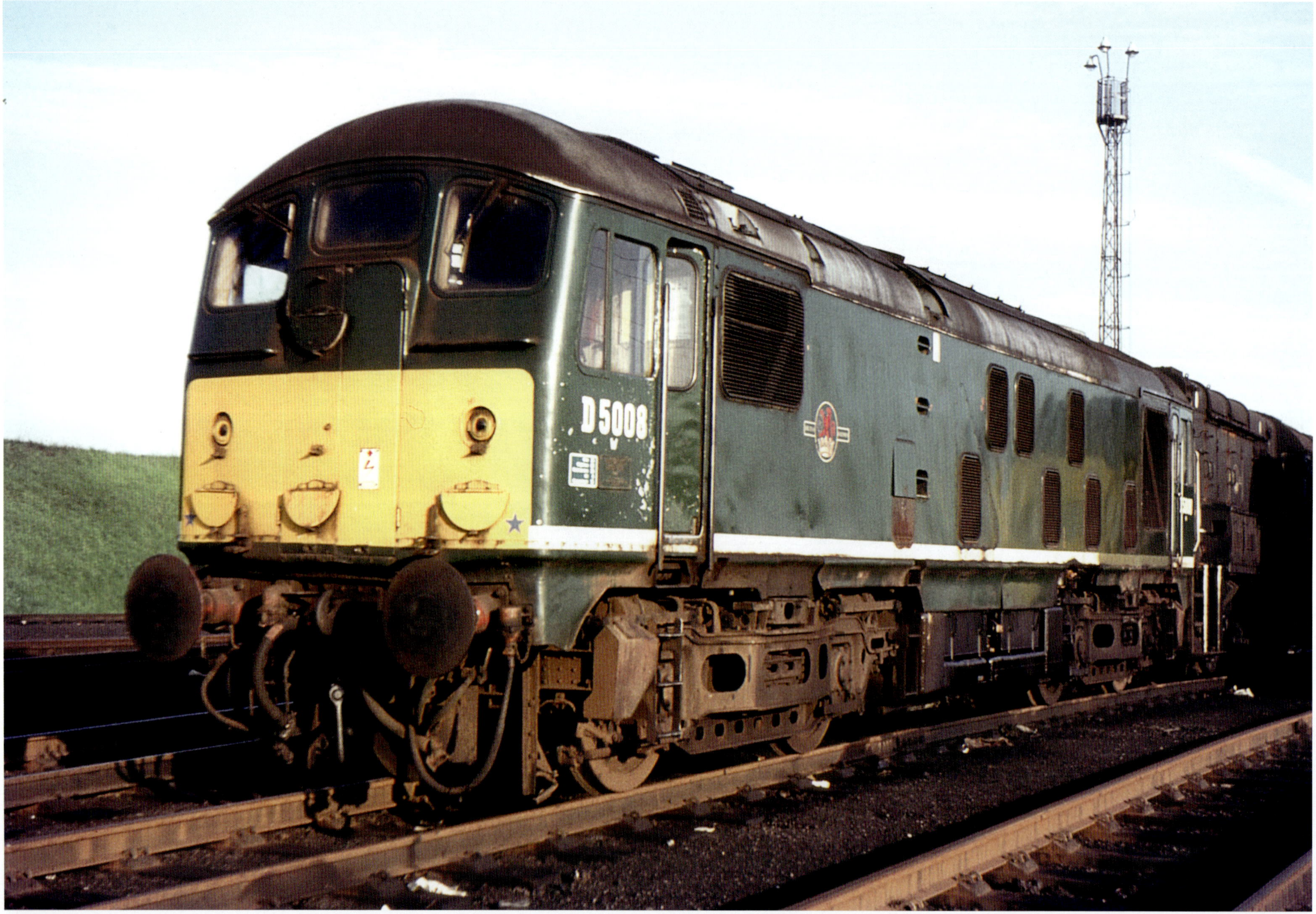
D5008

Not exactly common visitors, but this example was to be seen stabled at Tinsley depot sometime during 1969 with D5008 from the pool of Class 24s allocated to D05 the Crewe Division. Unlike one of Tinsley's long-term pets D3707 proudly wearing her 41A shed plate carefully painted along with her extra numbering, she is seen earning her keep attending to some light weight shunting in the marshalling yard sometime in 1967.
Both: *Dave Langham Collection*

Left: Likewise, smartly turned out by the Tinsley depot staff as today's motive power for a charter service for the former employees of this once large steelworks in Rotherham, the full yellow end of D1775 suggests this un-dated shot was taken around 1968-69 in the depot yard.

Right: Similarly, the fresh coat of yellow paint applied to D8064 stabled down in the yard's servicing area indicates this view is probably from early 1968. **Both: Dave Langham Collection**

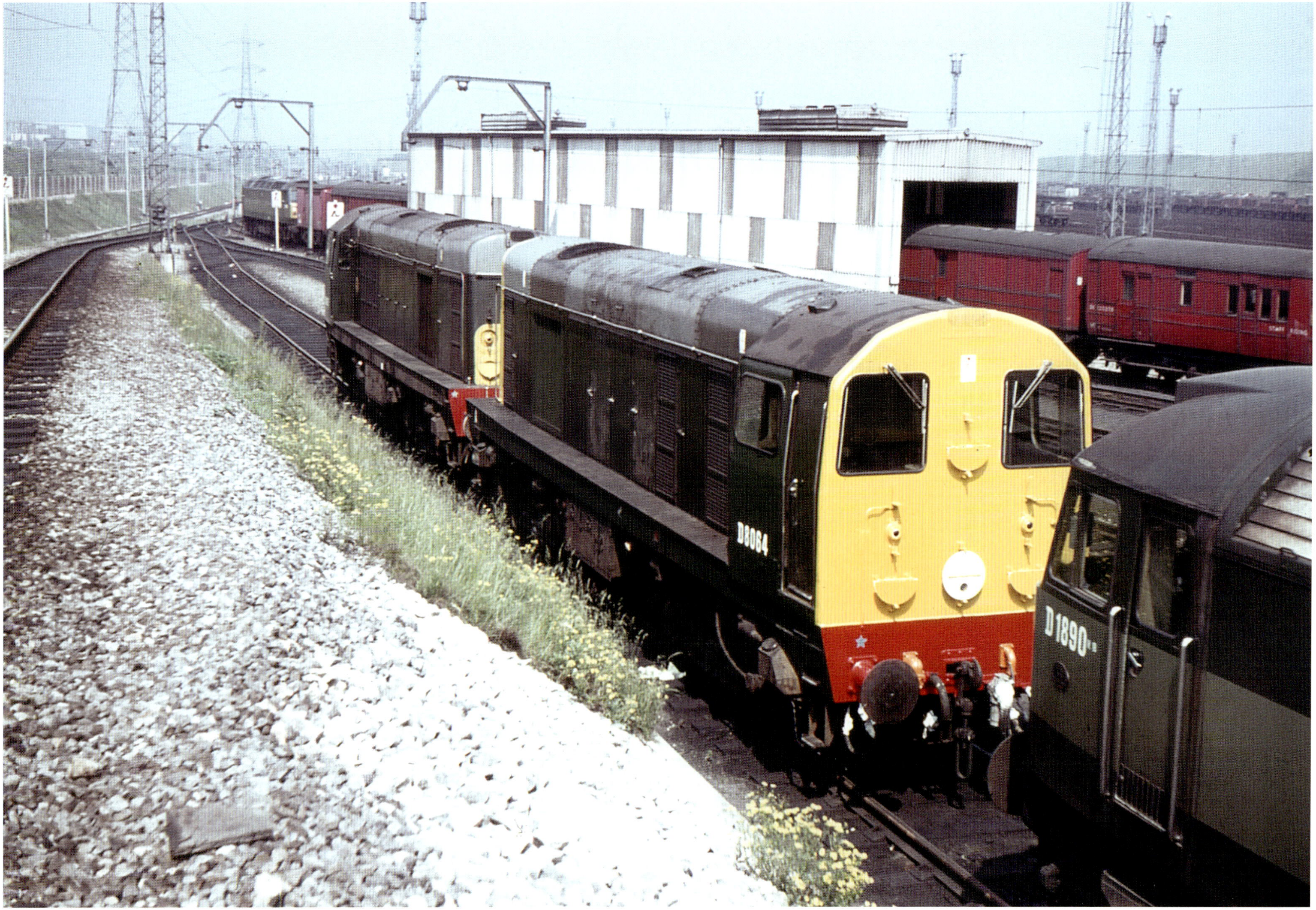
D8064
D1890

38

Between January 1966 and May 1970, Class 31, D5630 was allocated to 41A Tinsley, the fact that she appears to have been sent back home from a recent visit to Doncaster Works still carrying her D prefix, leads us to think this shot was taken in early 1968 as they have also applied a small set of InterCity arrows to her flanks too. A side view of the pet D3707 from around the same time, she was allocated to Tinsley in November 1964 very soon after the depot opened on 26 April 1964. *Both: Dave Langham Collection*

Taken just before its move away from Tinsley to join the fold at 32B Ipswich in August 1967, D6749 takes a breather in the yard of the maintenance depot. Sent to Sheffield's Darnall depot then coded as 41A when new, the move here coincided with the transfer of the shed code and the rundown of the city's Darnall depot as Tinsley opened in April 1964. Freshly returned from overhaul at Doncaster Works in early 1968, D5538 is spick and span both inside and outside posed for her portrait in the sunshine, but for how much longer once back to her regular duties? *Both: Dave Langham Collection*

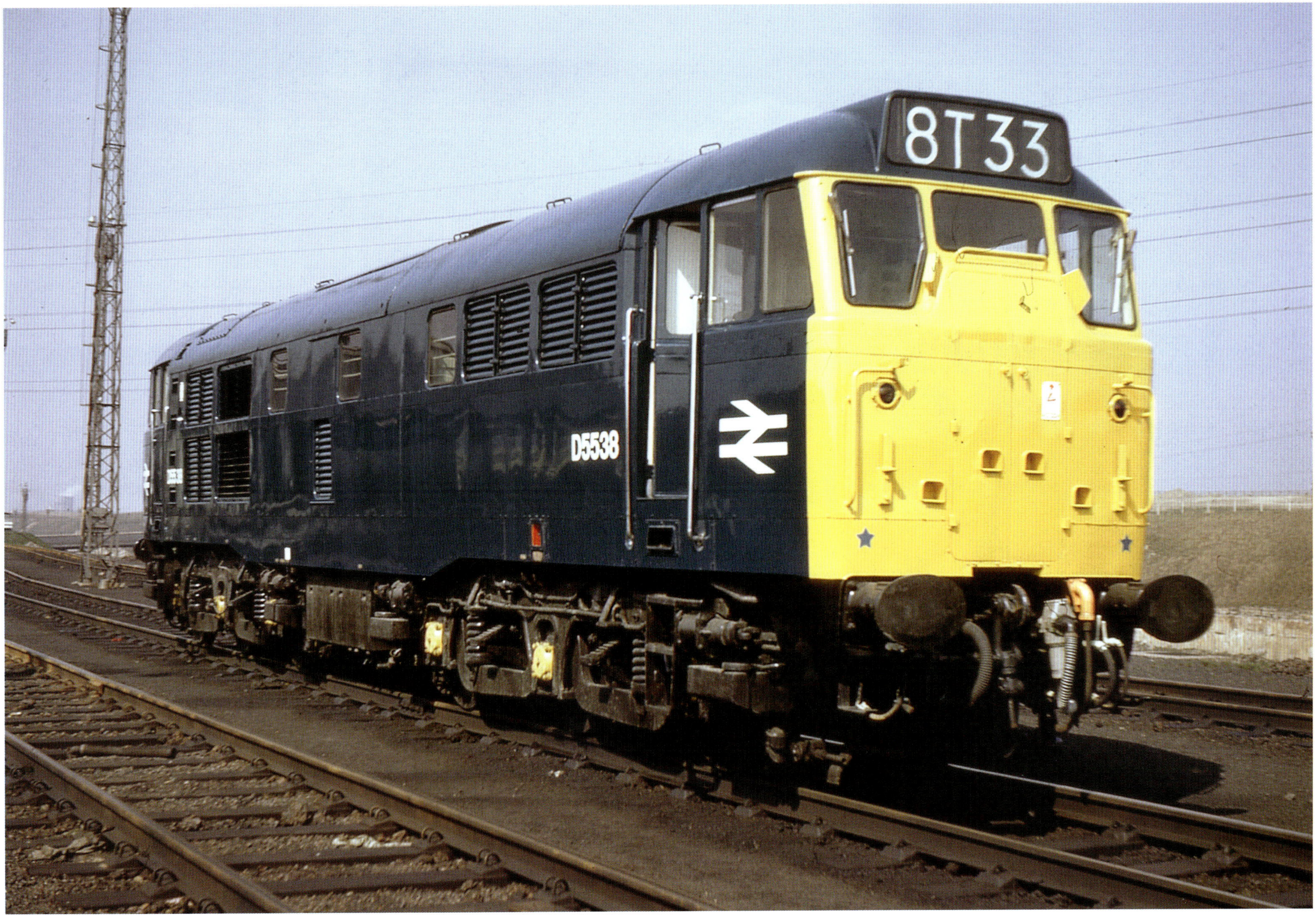
8T33
D5538

Blue is the Colour

Seen just as the sun is going down is another example of Doncaster Works applying fresh blue paintwork to D2072 newly transferred here to 55F Bradford Hammerton Street in early 1968 as attempts were being made to replace the DMU depot's allocation of Class 04 shunters with these Class 03s instead. An example of one of these soon to be withdrawn Drewry Class 04 shunters lurks inside the shed. *R.C.T.S. Archive*

Opposite: Wearing an early rendition of the proposed blue livery in a more satin finish without any visible British Railways emblems showing on this side at least was D58 The King's Own Royal Border Regiment when seen inside the maintenance shed at Cricklewood in the summer of 1969. The large, shed building here serviced both mainline locomotives and DMUs side by side. *Strathwood Library Collection*

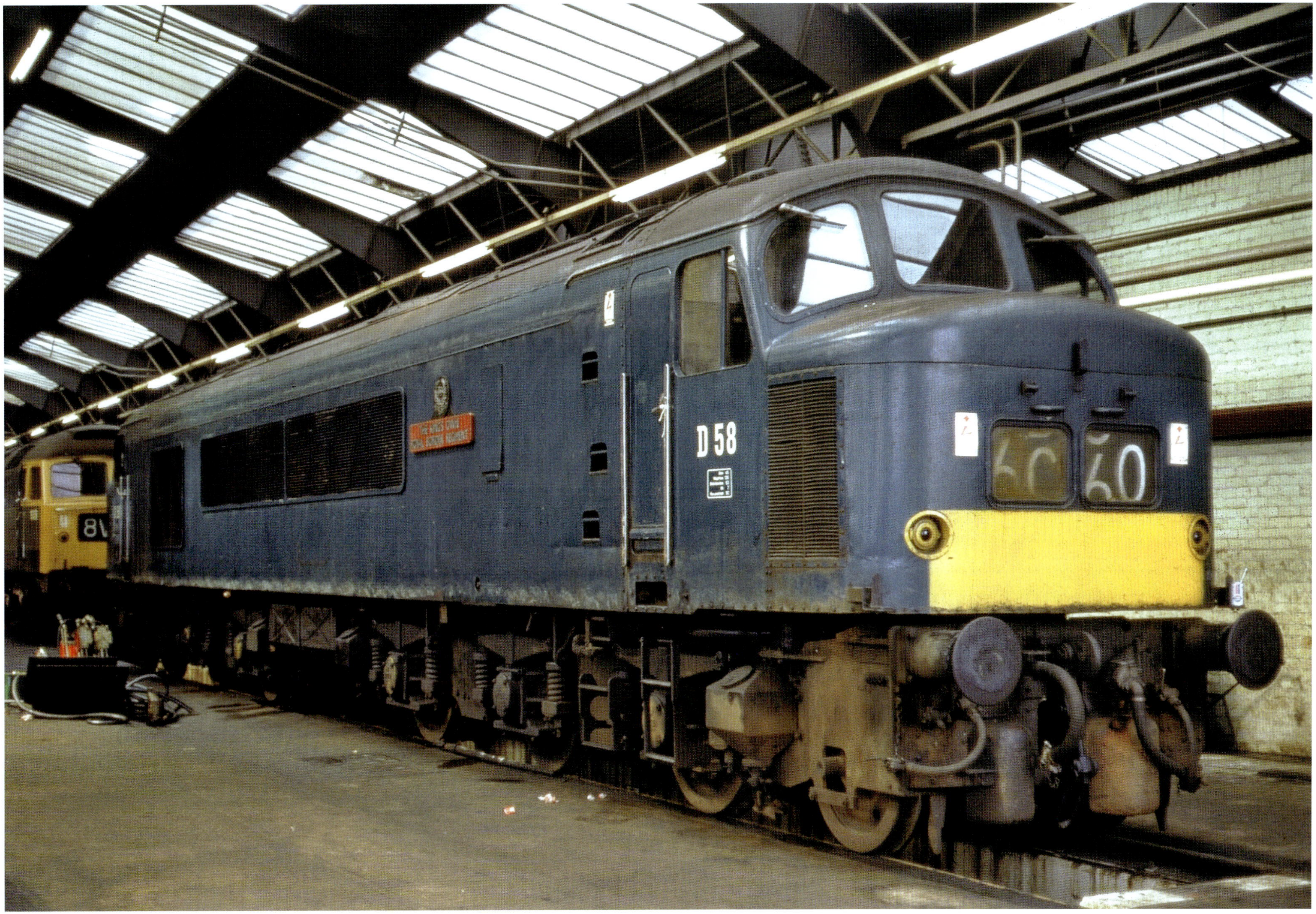
D 58
60

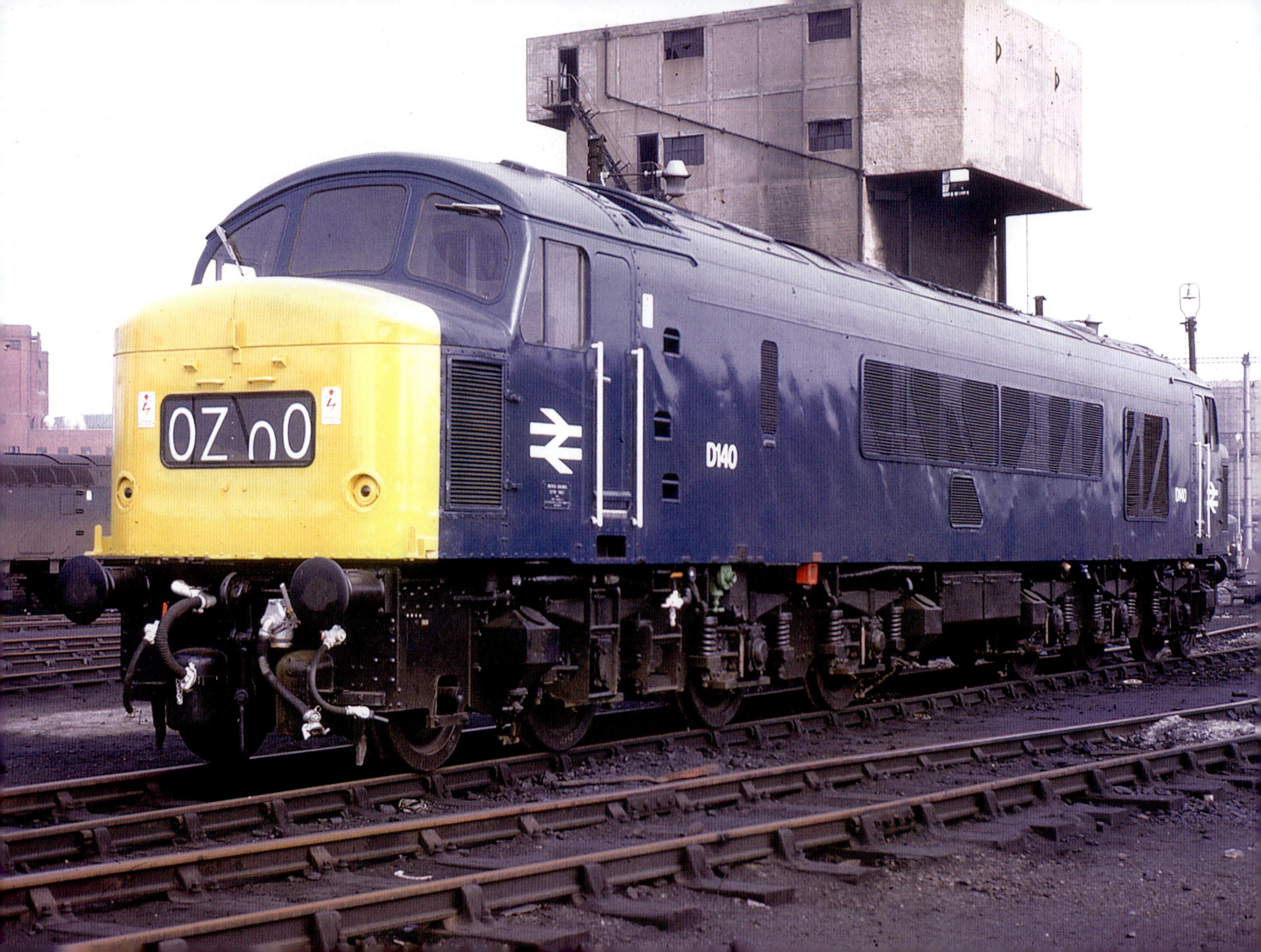
D140

Opposite: With the British Rail approved version of the corporate blue InterCity livery having just been applied within Derby Works, Class 46 Peak D140 stands proud ready for a return to traffic in the former steam shed yard in early February 1967. At this time, she would remain part of the LMML pool which morphed into D16 The Nottingham Division the following year, thus making her a regular along the former Midland Railway's routes. ***TOPticl***

When seen in the depot yard at Hither Green in August 1968, E6036 had been in service for just over two years since June 1966, however the smartness of her attire suggests she has been cleaned up for a recent head of state special working. The condition of sister locomotive E6038 behind was more normal at this point before the electro-diesel fleet came due for overhaul and a return to traffic in all over blue and yellow. ***Jonathan Martin***

Swindon Works had no sooner seized the chance to start painting Warships and Westerns into their preferred maroon livery, before British Rail's corporate blue became the order of the day for all locomotives leaving the works. After a number of locomotives going out with half yellow fronts, ex-works departures settled into this style worn by both Class 22s D6328 and D6326 sandwiching Hymek D7035 here at Old Oak Common around late July or early August 1967. Note the neatly stenciled shed allocations still in use before they gave way to stickers in 1968. Likewise, once again we can see the Western region's preferred use of colour spots to indicate route availability, a system Swindon carried over from steams days. *Rail Online*

When D1733 was cleaned up by staff at Old Oak Common for display at the Great Western Society arranged Open Day at Taplow on 17 September 1966, she had already lost the stick-on InterCity arrows with a red background on her cab sides. Judging from her appearance on the day, she has been smartened up a little with a pressure wash around her lower quarters and a swift coat of black paint, maybe to the roof as well. Although someone has taken some extra care and pride on the alloy 81A shed plate. Also, on display this day were D1030 Western Musketeer in an early version of blue and D837 Ramillies ex-works but in green. Representing the Great Western Society with steam, they had assembled 4079 Pendennis Castle, 7808 Cookham Manor and the Prairie tank 6106 to raise both funds and new members. *Grahame Wareham*

Left: The distinctive modernized premium image created to update the outdated burnt umber and cream livery previously associated with the Pullman Company initially would be this attractive Nanking blue and grey scheme upon the introduction of the five Pullman units in 1960 to a wave of publicity. The London Midland Region were allocated two six-car sets to work between St. Pancras and Manchester, while the Western Region had three eight-car sets for use between Paddington and Bristol, Birmingham, and South Wales. This view was taken a year or so after their introduction on the Western Region's Pullman service with an eight-car set heading for Birmingham at Ashendon Junction situated between Princes Risborough and Bicester.
Mike Morant Collection

The London Midland Region's electric locomotives were delivered in a somewhat similar style, with the shade of blue often described as electric blue in many publications. In this view we can see how the broken white was perhaps a poor choice unless the locomotives were regularly cleaned in everyday traffic. This duo is seen at Willesden soon after the start of the full electric working from Euston in May 1966, at the time E3172 was known as a Class AL6 and E3059 as a Class AL5. The first of this pair to be withdrawn would be E3059 as now a Class 85 numbered 85111 in March 1990, whereas E3172 would be sold out of service as 86233 as a Class 86 in February 2007 and sold to Bulgaria for further use in 2012.
Rail Online

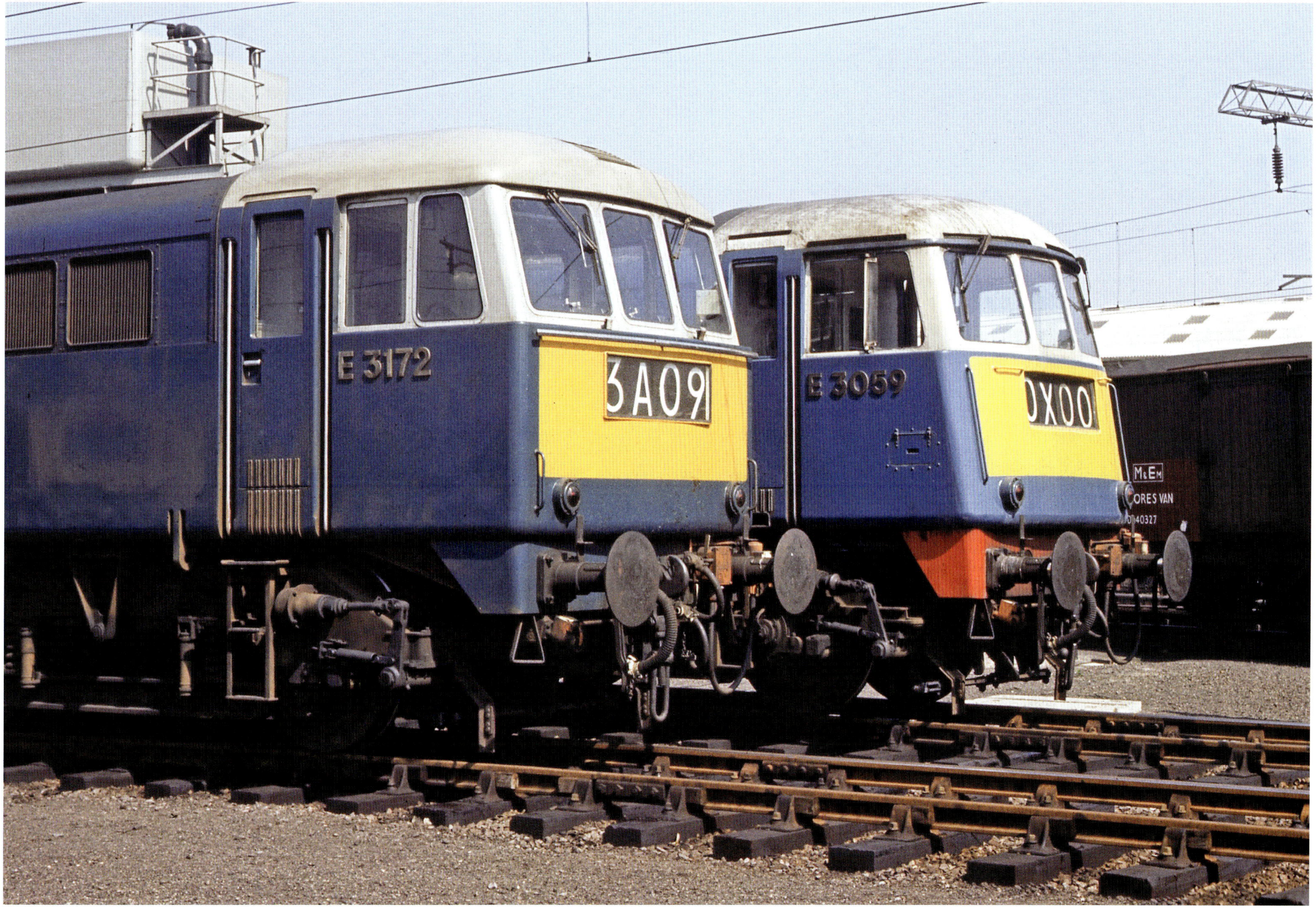
E 3172
3A09
E 3059
0X00

The switch from two tone green livery into blue first occurred for D9010 The King's Own Scottish Borderer during her general repairs and the fitting of dual braking completed in February 1968. Although she had been unique for a Deltic in carrying InterCity arrows since December 1966 whilst still in green. This view was taken upon her release for testing after another works visit for light repairs in late November and early December 1969. She is seen at Doncaster station still carrying her D prefix; however, these were later seen painted over very soon afterwards. *Dave Langham Collection*

Opposite: After acceptance testing took place at Crewe Works in March 1968, D412 then brand new and gloriously finished in her shiny blue livery from the Vulcan Foundry, took up service initially allocated to the LMWL pool, which soon became D05 The Crewe Division. Her first duties were a mix of crew training runs, express passenger and both parcels and goods traffic northwards from here at Crewe Diesel Depot where she now shows plenty of evidence of lots of use and extraordinarily little love and cleaning in her first year of service, as does one of her sister Class 50s stabled alongside that first autumn. *Dave Langham Collection*

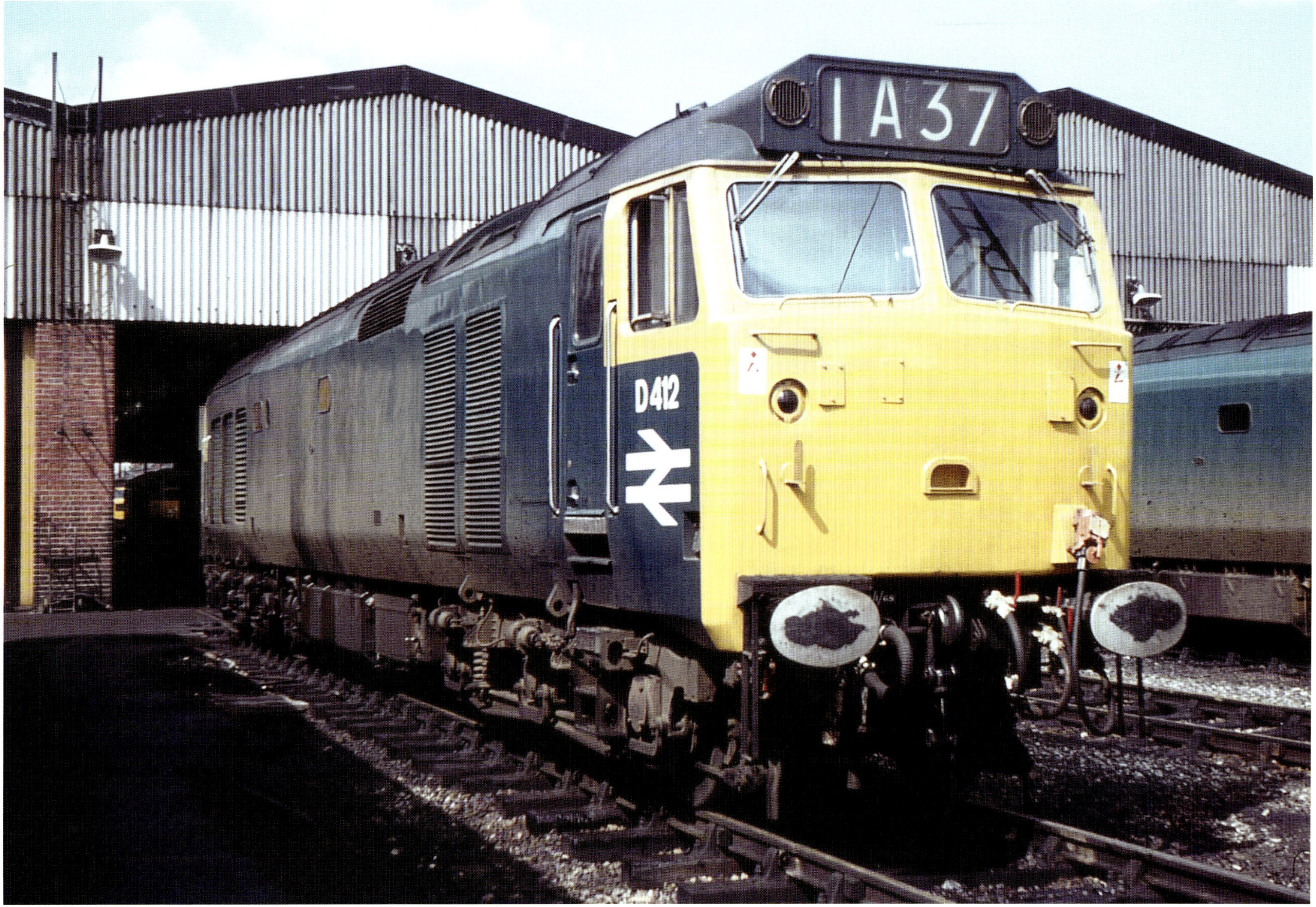
1A37
D412

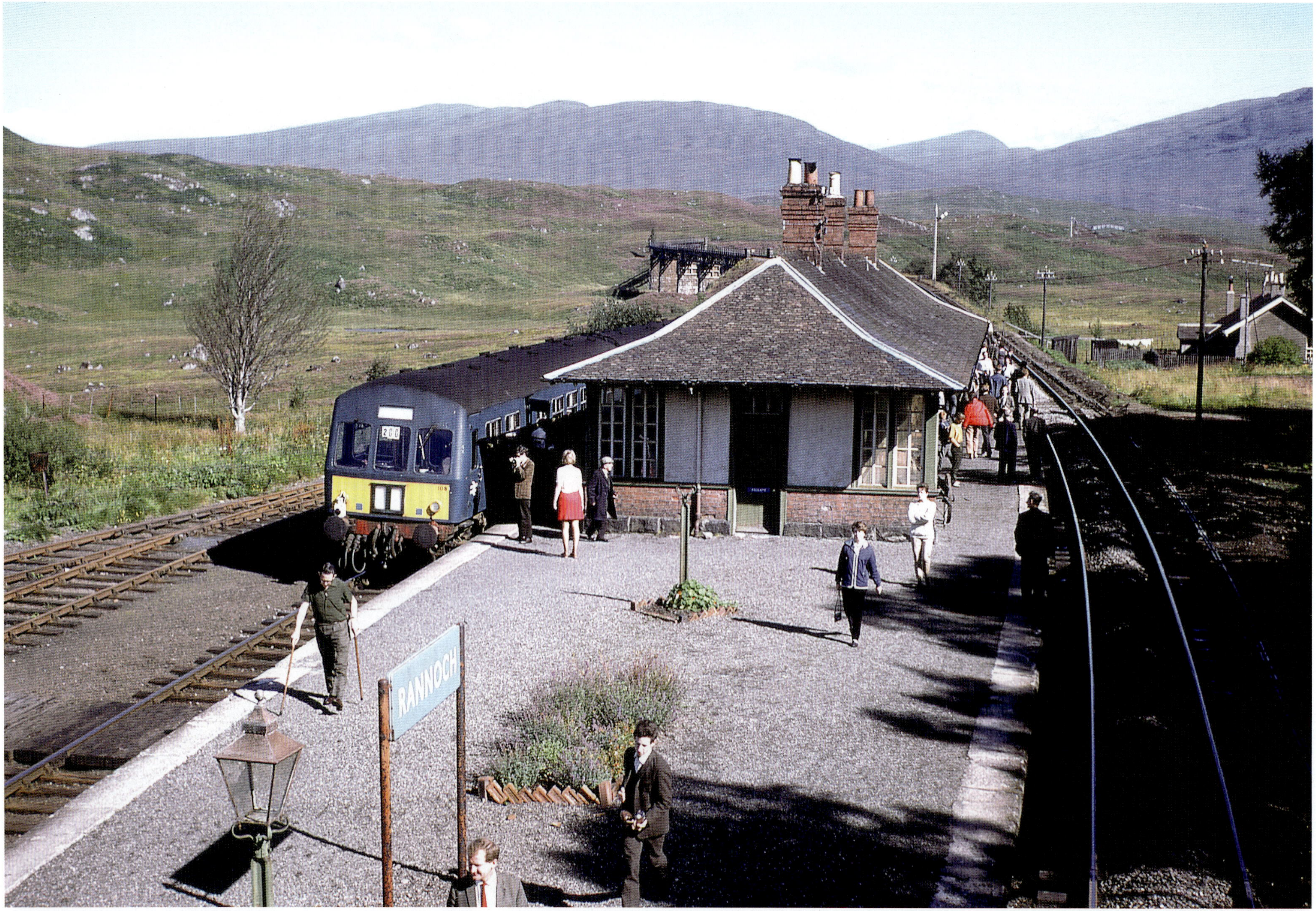
RANNOCH

Opposite: The arrival of a special on 24 August 1968 full of passengers has brought an almost rush hour crowd to the otherwise lonely and remote island platform at Rannoch, all accessed by the footbridge from where our photographer was standing. The Metropolitan-Cammell three-car DMU has brought members and guests of the Branch Line Society. The tour had begun at Glasgow Queen Street travelling to Fort William and onwards to Mallaig and back. *TOPticl*

Still wearing a clean appearance after its recent overhaul within Crewe Works, 1505 has returned to service in the new corporate blue livery, minus the D prefix post August 1968. The use of just one set of InterCity arrows worn amidships was now the norm, rather than using two sets per side with one under each cab window. Photographed here during 1969 making a stop with an up service at Doncaster. ***Dave Langham Collection***

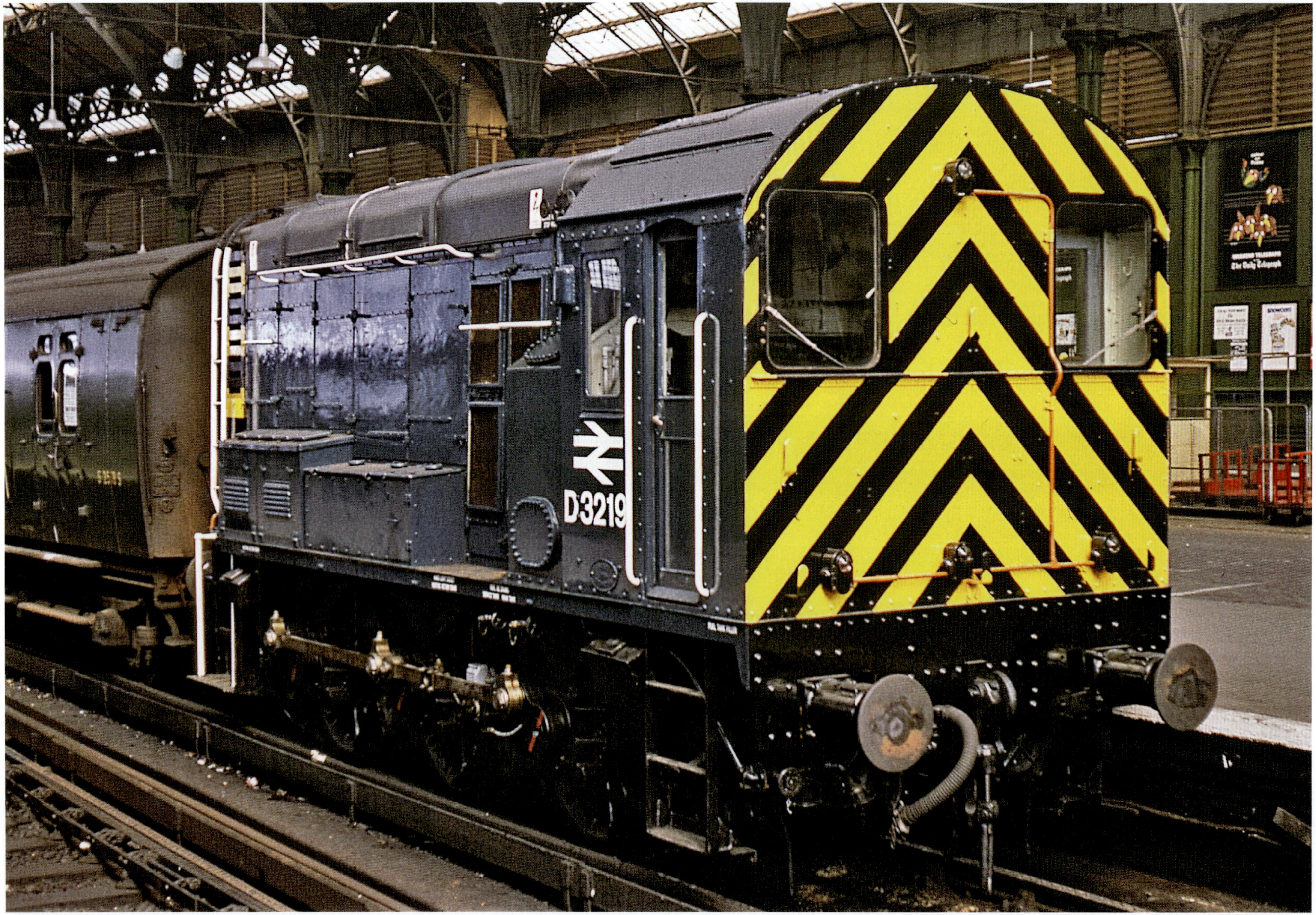
D3219

Opposite: One of Eastleigh Works' earliest interpretations of the new livery was applied to D3219, and the shunter was released back into service at 75A Brighton in March 1967. Soon afterwards it caught the attention of our cameraman while it was on duty as the seaside town's station pilot. *Colour Rail*

Still very much on trial to see how the initially proposed paint scheme held up in regular service D5578 shows off her unique livery for a Brush Type 2 on shed at Stratford on 7 April. The half yellow front had been applied the previous year which certainly lifted this colour scheme. *Colour Rail*

This was the short-lived early version of blue utilizing two InterCity arrows as applied to only thirteen other Class 47s as they came due for overhauls at Crewe Works between November 1967 and August 1968. Many Class 47s only requiring minor works repairs during this period returned to service just with their two-tone green paint touched up. This shot of D1723 was taken at the Crewe North stabling point early in 1969. ***Dave Langham Collection***

Opposite: Wolverton Works would have overhauled this Class AM5/1 three-car set and released it in this blue livery interpretation sometime during 1967. By the time of this shot being taken at Walthamstow in September 1968 it was already beginning to look work weary from endless runs back and forth from Liverpool Street to Chingford or Enfield. One thing noticeable in compiling this selection is the fact that just how few photographers took any notice of these units. ***TOPticl***

Eastern Electrics

One of the earliest uses of a yellow warning panel to help protect trackside workers away from shunting locomotives, was applied to this Class AM6 unit whose usual employment would be on the Liverpool Street to Gidea Park and Shenfield services. But on this occasion is heading for Ilford having worked to Clacton-on-Sea most likely on test. In the background a brand-new Class AM5/1 unit is stored awaiting acceptance into service during May 1960.
Colour Rail

Although one-hundred-and-twelve of these four-car Class AM2 sets were built for the Fenchurch Street to Shoeburyness routes, very few colour photographs seem to have been taken of them either in the sixties or the seventies, making this scene at Shenfield around 1961 a real rarity. *Colour Rail*

The stylish Class AM9 EMUs introduced for the express workings from here at Liverpool Street to Clacton-on-Sea and Walton-on-the-Naze were unique for multiple units wearing maroon livery. This would soon change as units fell due for overhaul at Wolverton Works after the early months of 1967 as blue and grey livery would be applied, but on 25 July 1966 set number 627 was the lead in this departure from the capital. *Peter Simmonds*

Sixty-five outer suburban Class AM7 and AM8 units were built numbered 101 to 132 and 133 to 165 to cover duties such as stopping services from here at Clacton-on-Sea to Colchester. The unit on the right is stabled in a bay on 27 March 1966 as another can be glimpsed in traffic beyond the recently arrived Class AM9 express units. *Colour Rail*

Two of the then brand new three-car EMU sets ordered from York's Holgate Road Carriage Works await consignment from York to their intended route to serve the busy Liverpool Street-Enfield-Chingford commuter lines in 1960. Fifty-five of these sets would finally be delivered and once again scarcely photographed by enthusiasts during their service lives. *Colour Rail*

The North Eastern Railway was to be considered very progressive when they began to electrify several of Newcastle-upon-Tyne's suburban railways from 1904 at 600v dc. Tracing its history back to those early days was this Motor Parcels Van DE900729 parked up near Gateshead on 13 January 1963, this was one of two such units converted to de-icing units and later withdrawn in 1966. *Colour Rail*

Below: Two further parcels' units covered the North Tyneside system numbered E29467E and this one E29468E which is seen with a single wagon in tow near Trafalgar yard. Both were built by Metropolitan Cammell in 1938 and were made redundant by June 1967 when the system was dieselized. *Colour Rail*

Having just arced its leading pick-up shoe a small puff of smoke can be seen as this two-car unit sets off from Manors station on 21 May 1962. Each of the sixty-four units was formed of a Motor Driving Coach and Driving Trailer. In addition to the two Motor Parcels Vans there were also two Motor Luggage Vans numbered E29165E and E29166E on the once busy system. *R.C.T.S. Archive*

A four-coach working is seen from the footbridge at Manors on 13 June 1964. The articulated layout of the units can be seen, this means of reducing the number of bogies in carriage sets was favoured by the former LNER on a number of their locomotive hauled four and five coach sets. The third rail and overhead wiring serving the Quayside branch and the two Class ES1 locomotives on the system would see very little if any further use from this point as both locomotives were withdrawn on 14 September the same year. As we can see in our next view on the platforms at Newcastle Central the system was often expected to carry a wealth of mail and parcels traffic as another four-car working prepares to set off on 8 May 1965. *Both: Colour Rail*

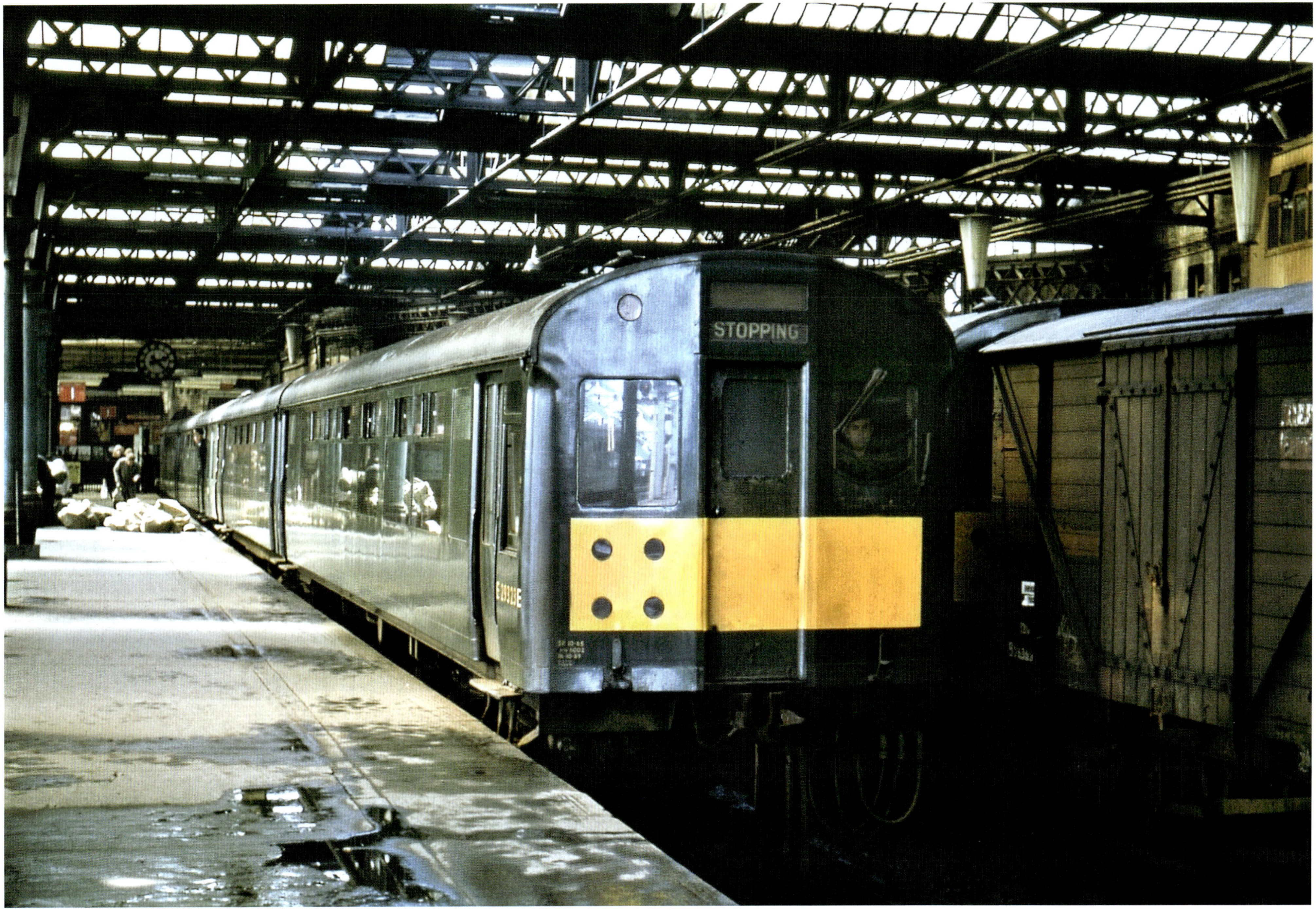
STOPPING

The two Class ES1 locomotives were a familiar sight working the heavily graded Quayside line from Heaton since their construction in 1902, having been introduced to reduce the problems of smoke within the tunnel on the branch using steam locomotives. In early British Railways days, the pair wore a plain black livery, however with consideration to their historical importance, they were repainted to reflect the lined apple green livery of the long since defunct North Eastern Railway who had introduced them, during their final few years in service. Sandwiched between two of the diesel shunters that would soon oust both 26500 and 26501 the former shows off her livery and the original NER crest too in this view taken at Heaton in July 1962. Likewise, 26501 shows off her ability also to collect the juice from the overhead sections installed on part of the route in this second scene near the quayside on 7 May 1962.
Photos: Colour Rail & R.C.T.S. Archive

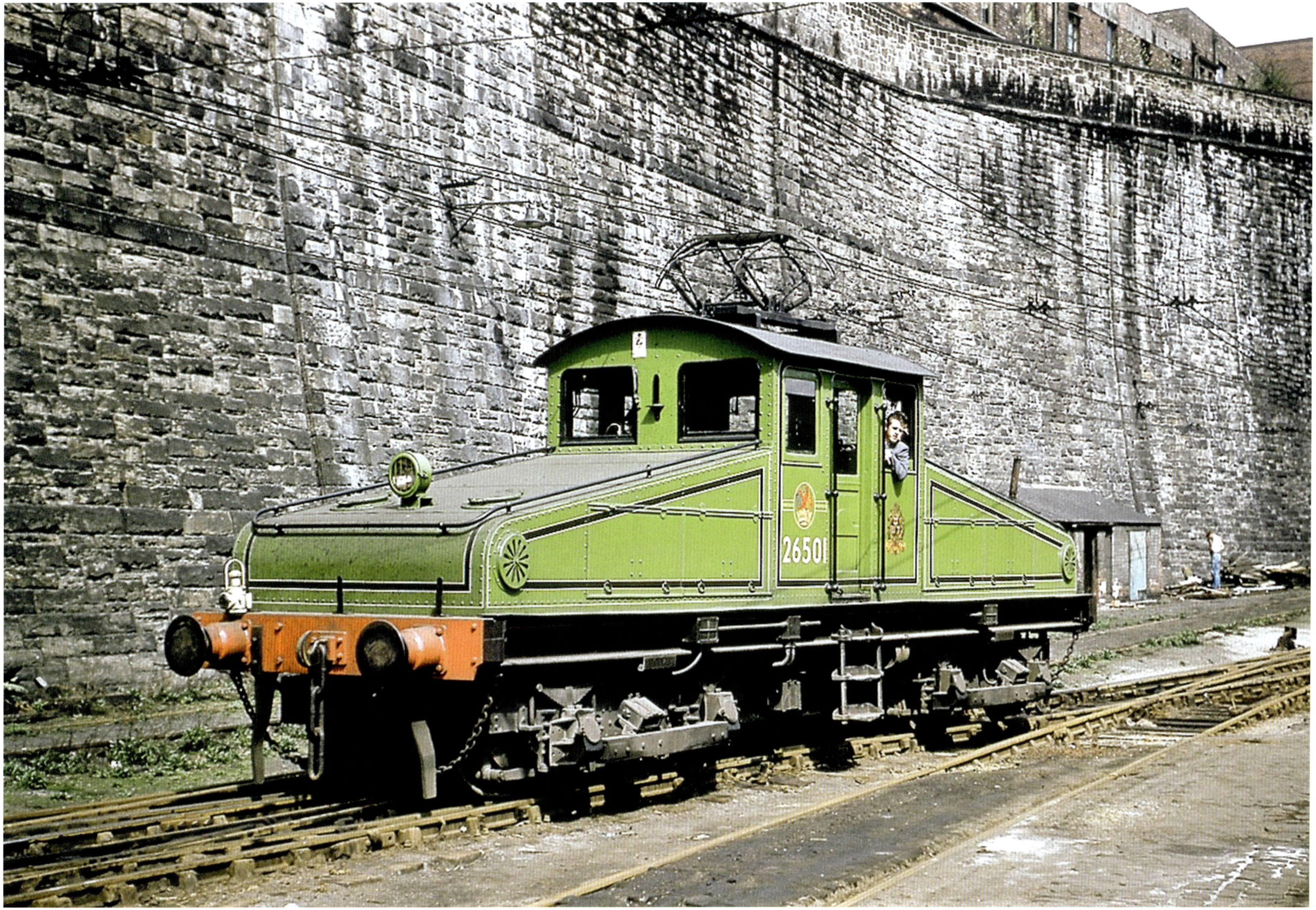
26501

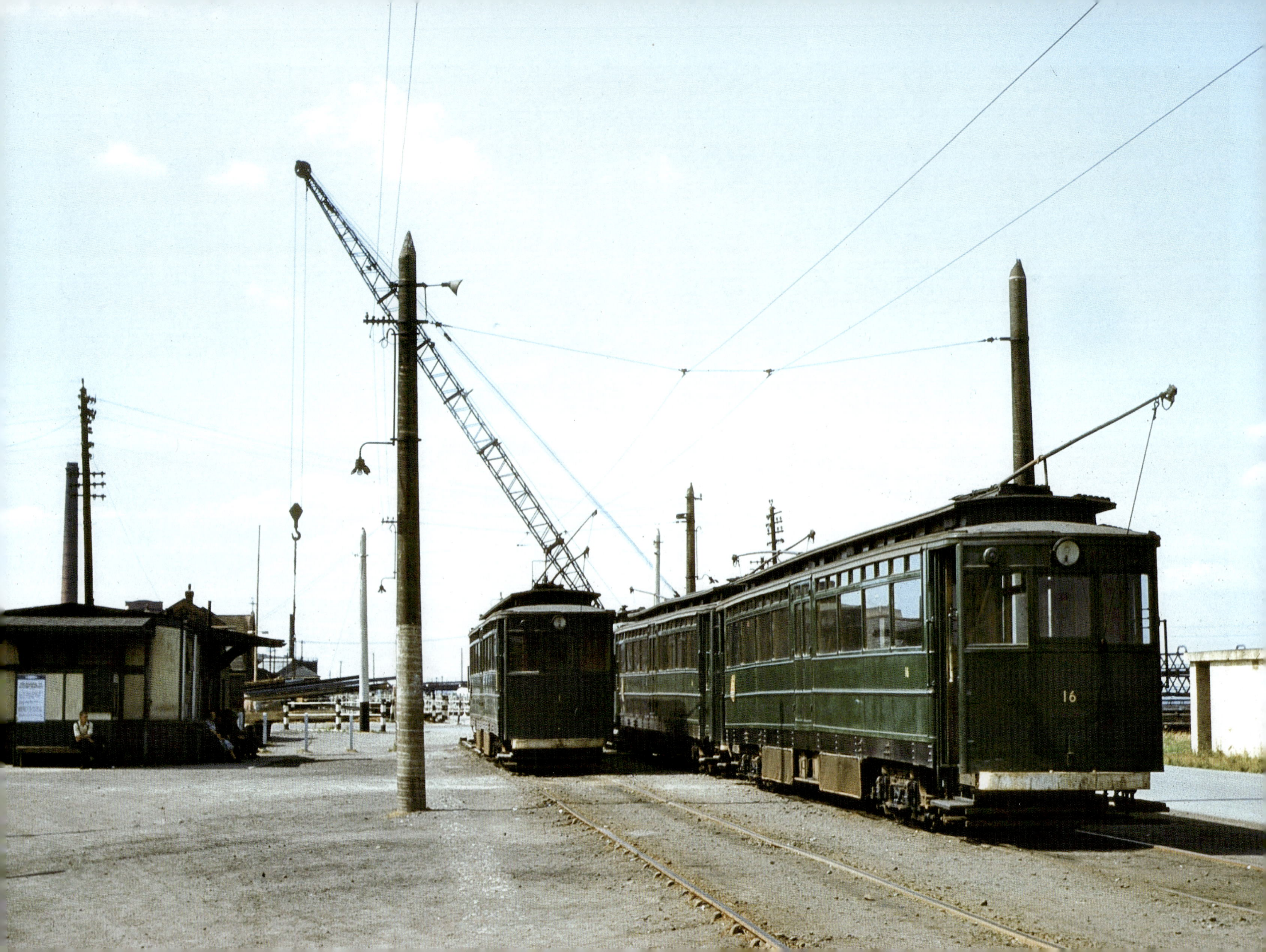
16

Another early forward-thinking venture in electrification was applied by the former Great Central Railway linking Grimsby and Immingham in 1912. The line was equipped with trams to provide easy transport for workers to the extremely busy port and docks complexes. In 1923 the line was duly absorbed into the LNER at the grouping and then passed to British Railways in 1948. Power to the trams was supplied at 500v dc with a depot established at Pyewipe. The scene opposite was taken showing three of the later build longer cars with their characteristic sagging frames on 26 July 1959. Brush Electrical Engineering Co. Ltd of Loughborough initially supplied cars 1-4 which were Britain's longest trams at 54ft 2in long. These were mounted on Brush Standard 4ft 6in wheelbase trucks with Dick Kerr DK9 50hp motors on the inner axles. Dick Kerr DB1 K4 controllers were fitted with rheostatic and magnetic braking. The cars could take 32 passengers on reversible seats, 8 on tip-up seats, and about 30 additional standing passengers. Here we have car no. 1 seen at Pyewipe Depot after the cessation of services in July 1961. *Photos: Strathwood Library Collection & Brian Mennie/Rail Photoprints*

British Railways also purchased three single deck maximum-traction air-braked bogie trams from Newcastle Corporation in 1948. These were the only Grimsby & Immingham trams to have upholstered seats. They were followed in 1951 by nineteen single deck trams purchased from the Gateshead & District Tramways Company numbered as 17-33. One of these replaced the No. 5 Works Car and became DE320224 seen opposite. A second tram was damaged when a crane fell on it during unloading, and never entered service. The Eastern Region modified the Gateshead trams by adding a second lamp, re-profiling the wheels, and disconnecting the anti-runback feature on the controller. The Newcastle trams numbered as 6-8 appear to have been a stopgap feature only and were withdrawn in 1953 - shortly after the Gateshead trams entered service. Both photographs were taken at Pyewipe depot in the early summer of 1961. *Photos: Brian Mennie/Rail Photoprints & Strathwood Library Collection*

71

At its height of use in British Railways ownership the line saw 1,350,000 passenger journeys per annum in 1948. Proposals to close the route and the supply of replacement buses were progressively made during the 1950s and the service was finally withdrawn on 1 July 1961. Even at closure it was still handling around 250,000 passengers a year. This scene was taken on that final day as tram enthusiasts and locals alike enjoyed their last rides on the line. *Colour Rail*

Opposite: Having started its working career in the east end of London in February 1958 based out of 1D Devons Road, D8018 remained there after the shed code changed to 1J in September 1963. The depot near Bow closed completely on 10 February 1964, which initiated a short move to the nearby depot at 30A Stratford, performing much the same duties as before such as this local breakdown train working, passing through Stratford's mainline station on its way back to the depot the same year. *Colour Rail*

Under the Wires

Another design of Type 1 associated with both Devons Road, and Stratford depots were the British Thomson Houston 800hp Bo-Bo locomotives. On 6 October 1962 D8236 found itself rostered to head this five coach RCTS organized tour around a number of east London's recently closed goods and passenger routes for as far as it could travel along their tracks, this included the Silvertown Tramway. The tour set off from here at Liverpool Street at 13.36 covering eighty-eight miles by its return at 18.51. *Strathwood Library Collection*

Colour images of diesel and electric traction around the Essex countryside are also rarely found, making this one of Brush Type 2 D5619 from 30A Stratford depot taken only a few months after its introduction in the summer of 1960 an interesting find. Most of the rolling stock is a mix of British Railways Mark 1 suburban coaches with what appears to be a Gresley or Thompson vehicle towards the middle. The location for the shot is near Leigh-on-Sea on the former London, Tilbury & Southend Railway's route to the Essex coast. *Colour Rail*

In their early years of service, English Electric Type1s such as D8112 from 65A Eastfield could sometimes find themselves working passenger services, such as here at Jordan Hill on the electrified route from Hyndland in the Glasgow suburbs on 24 September 1965 substituting for a Blue Train when the power was off. Opposite we find one those distinctive Blue Trains with Sc75750 a Driving Trailer Second Open leading into Balloch around 1960, just before they were given set numbers on their front ends. *Photos: Colour Rail & Rail Online*

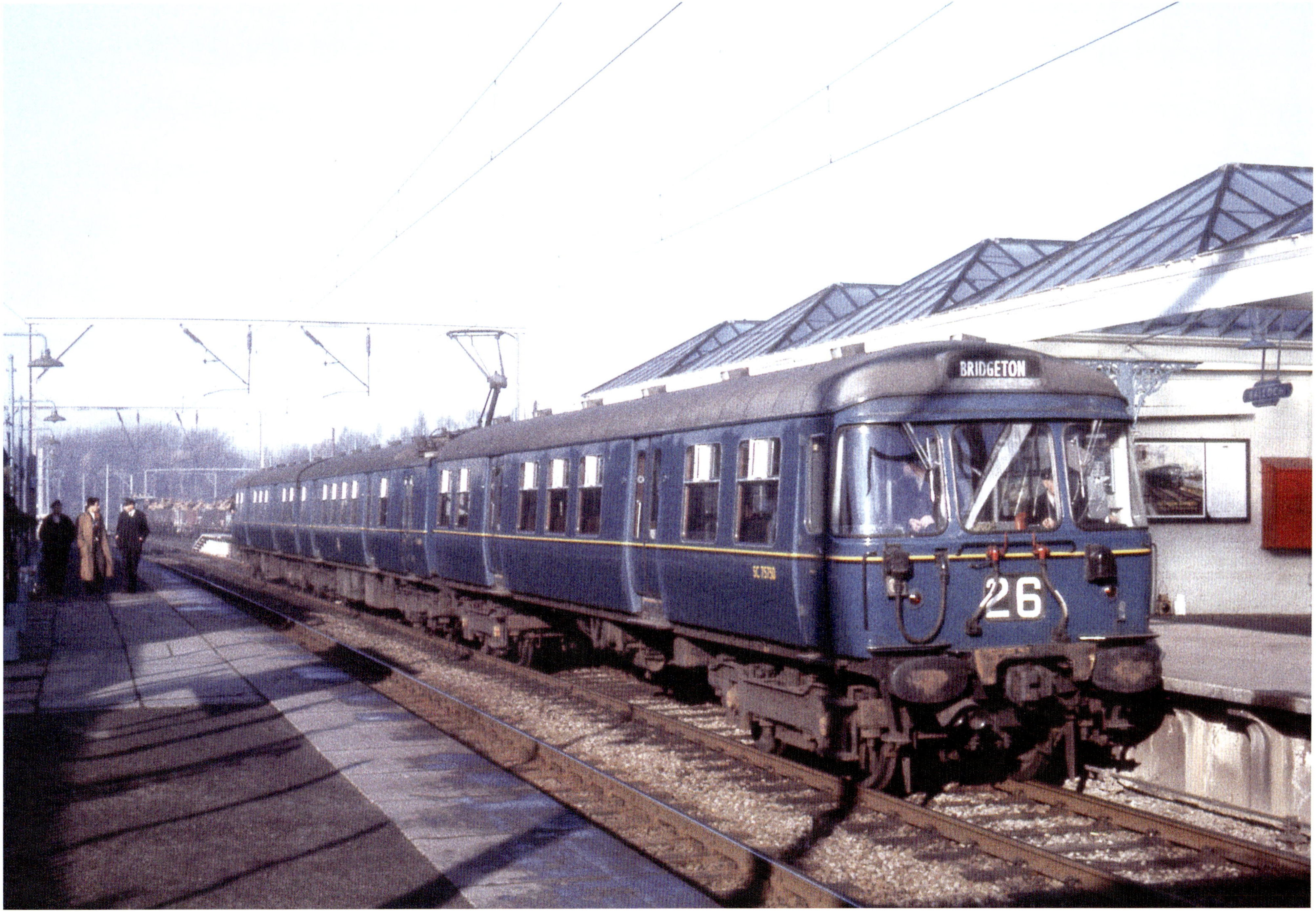

BRIDGETON
26

78

Off to the West Midlands next as the overhead wires begin appearing and changing the landscape there as well. In this view at Stafford, we have D211 Mauretania having a quite easy duty working this lightly loaded down freight during August 1966. Not too far away a couple of months beforehand on 26 May the same year the 17.25 Rugby Midland to Birmingham New Street service was in the hands of this smartly attired Park Royal twin unit. These were in fact built in Stockport at the former works of Crossley Motors Ltd who were also part of the AEC group at the time of construction in 1957, rather than Park Royal as the name suggests. *Photos: David Ford Snr & R.C.T.S. Archive*

The filthy appearance of D336 as part of the LNWL pool of locomotives based upon Crewe Diesel Depot does truly little to further the fresh new and efficient image being put forward by the advertising department of British Rail in this mid-sixties view of freight traffic at Coventry. Likewise, although there is plenty of evidence to show the arrival of the new electrified age here as well at Nuneaton on 31 August 1964, there is still some way to go as Class AL5 E3064 keeps company with some rolling stock from the former LMS and a Class 8F still active on freight in the background.
Photos: R.C.T.S. Archive & Colour Rail

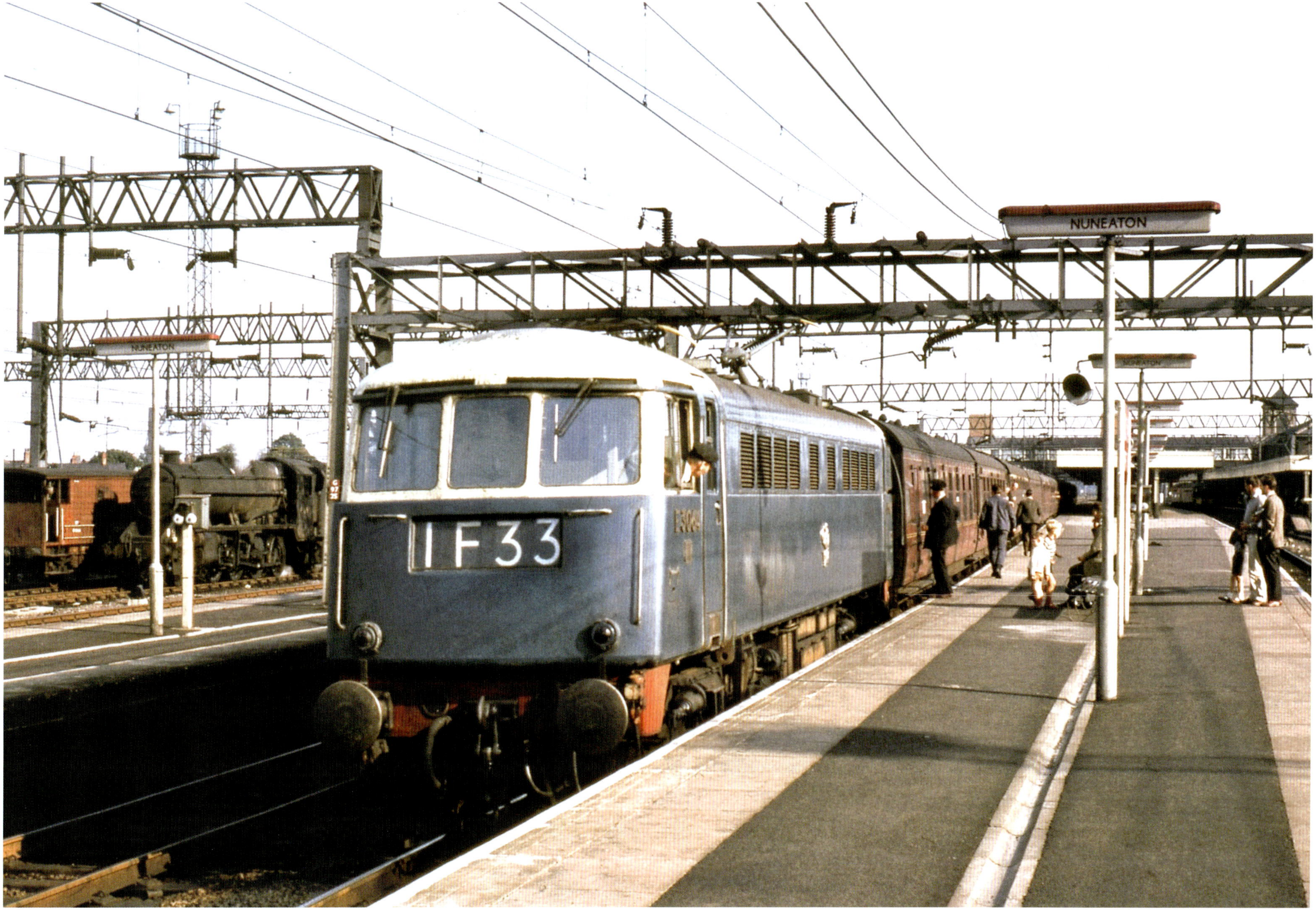
NUNEATON
NUNEATON
1F33

Things were not so different a year beforehand with an ex-LNER Thompson coach tucked in behind Class AL3 E3030 making a stop at Crewe, although in this instance they do indeed present a much cleaner appearance to the travelling public. The kind of mixed goods revenue shown opposite would hang on a while longer against the ever-stronger tide of road transport along the expanding motorway network which would in time become the norm for the transportation of everyday goods traffic. This was the scene at Stockport Edgeley station in early 1968 as steam's demise in the north west has recently handed these duties over to the likes of this Class AL5 E3060. *Both: R.C.T.S. Archive*

83

Staying within Cheshire we find ourselves back alongside the then much busier Crewe station, standing on the access road that led down the west side of the station to the diesel depot, which we are sure many readers will be familiar with. On 5 March 1967, D3083 was on duty as one of the station pilots, duties previously performed by ex-LMS Class 3F Jinties until a short while beforehand. The twenty-nine-year career of D3083 began in October 1954, with the shunter being first allocated to 16A Nottingham subsequent allocations aside from here at Crewe would revolve around Longsight, Springs Branch, Newton Heath, Saltley and finally Tyseley. Where upon arriving, it was promptly withdrawn even though the depot had taken the trouble to renumber it from 08068 to TYSELEY 1, it seems they never used it so in late 1984 it headed off for scrapping at Swindon Works instead. *R.C.T.S. Archive*

It is thought that the 1V29 Motorail service was heading for Newton Abbot as it was seen approaching Crewe station on 1 June 1969, with Class 50 D413 doing the honours thus far on this day. Closer inspection of the rear of the train only confirms just two cars being transported for their owner's holidays in the West Country on this occasion. Hopefully, the carriages are carrying a lot more paying passengers who preferred to use public transport or to walk while vacationing at a time when very few people had the opportunity to hire cars. **The KDH Archive**

Still within the transition into the rail blue years towards the 1970s, Class 85 E3071 has gained full yellow cab fronts, but still sports the original cast alloy lion & wheel emblems to complement those original raised numbers. When this shot was taken towards the south of Polesworth on 24 August 1968, one or two maroon Mark I coaches could still be seen within express formations, such as today's 09.40 Perth to Euston. It would be into the following decade before all the Class 40s would be wearing full yellow ends. This is D217 Carinthia in the center road at Stoke-on-Trent on Saturday 28 October 1967 with what might well be Cockshute Depot's breakdown train in tow. **Photos: R.C.T.S. Archive & John Ireland**

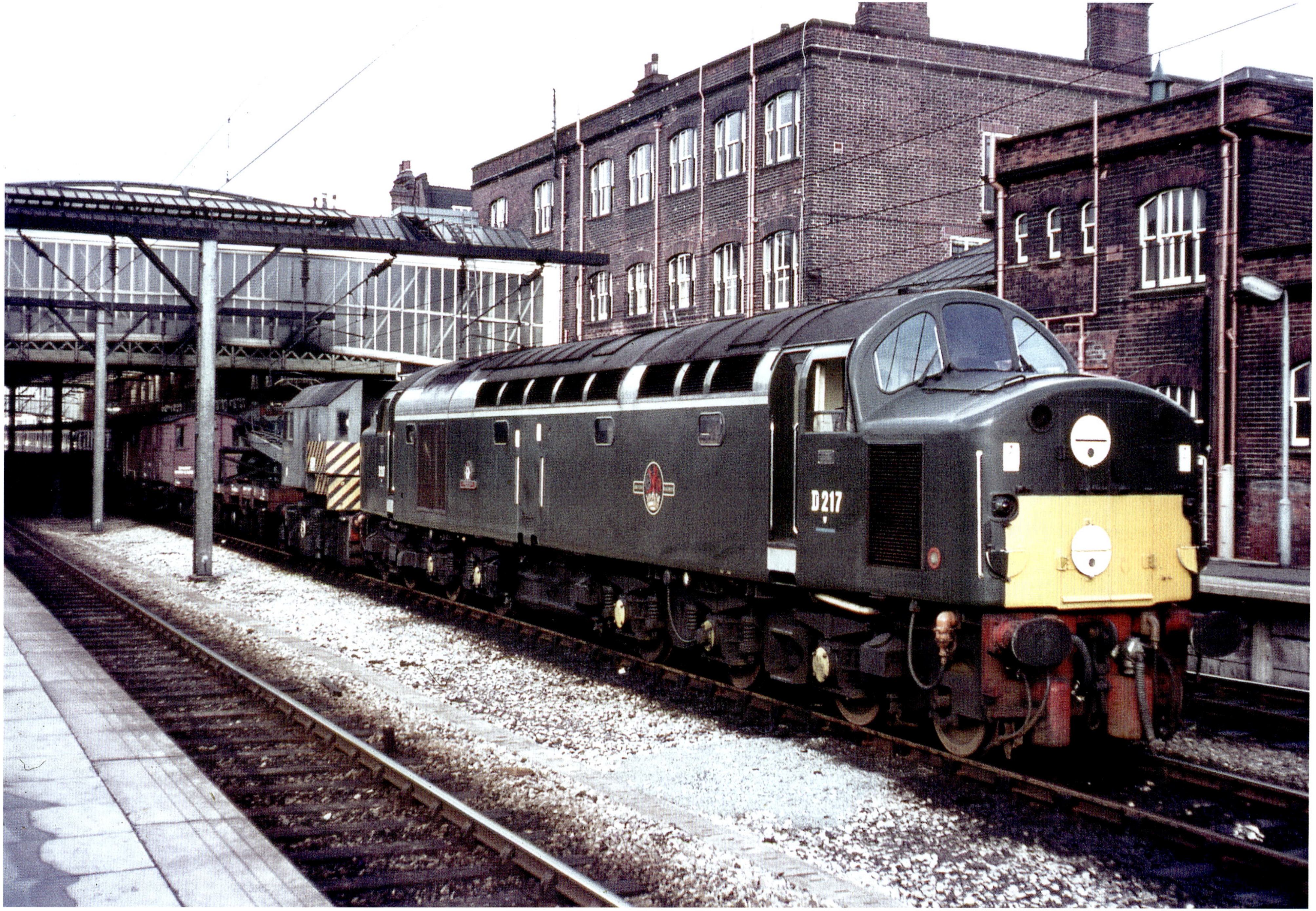
D217

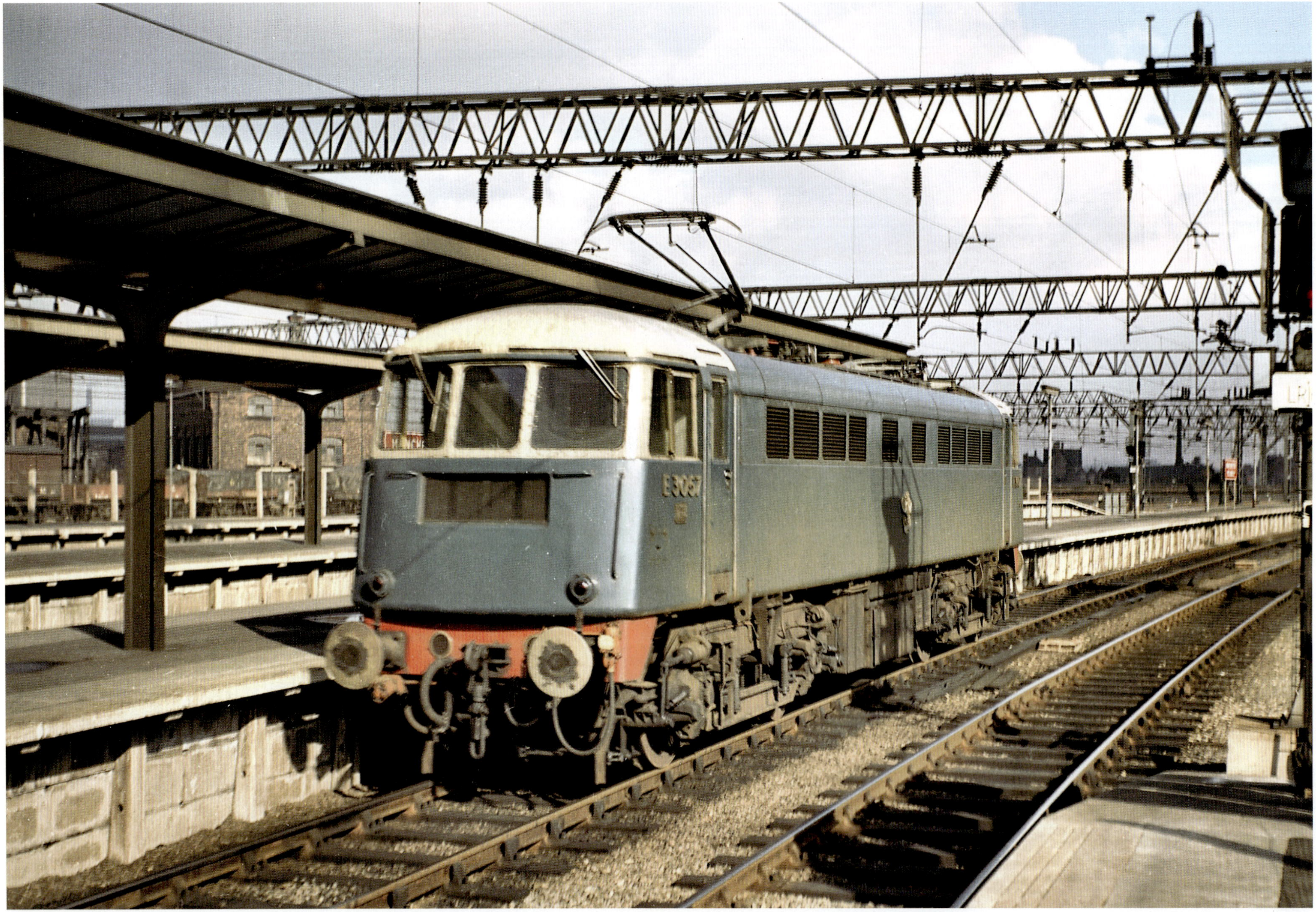
E3057

An undated image of E3057 light engine at Manchester Piccadilly station, she had been delivered new as the second built of her type as a Class AL5 from Doncaster Works on 3 June 1961. The numeric first of the class E3056 not arriving onto the London Midland Region until 19 August two months later, due to technical problems. This image was most likely taken around 1963. Whereas two builders were responsible for the construction of the 100 strong members of Class AL6, later known as Class 86 locomotives. Once again British Rail at Doncaster Works were given the job of completing 60 locomotives, while Vulcan Foundry was to build 40 as well. Eventually the numbers were reversed with English Electric at Vulcan Foundry building the majority due to capacity problems at Doncaster. When first introduced the AL6s built at Doncaster featured red buffer beams and those including E3172 seen here at Crewe on 30 April 1966 built at the Vulcan Foundry were delivered in Rail Blue as a straightforward way to tell them apart without their numbers.

Photos: Mike Morant Collection & John Ireland

Fresh from Crewe Works and a new one the for the spotters to cop in their notebooks was D1610 seen running light through Crewe's station roads on 22 August 1964. She would soon head to 87E Landore depot to take up her first allocation in her shiny new paintwork. Conversely, the early version of electric blue paintwork always seemed to have a duller sheen to it, that only became worse in traffic, as witnessed upon E3165 and E3082 in the depot yard at Willesden during 1966, it was never going to be practical with a white roof in service was it? *Photos: Colour Rail & Strathwood Library Collection*

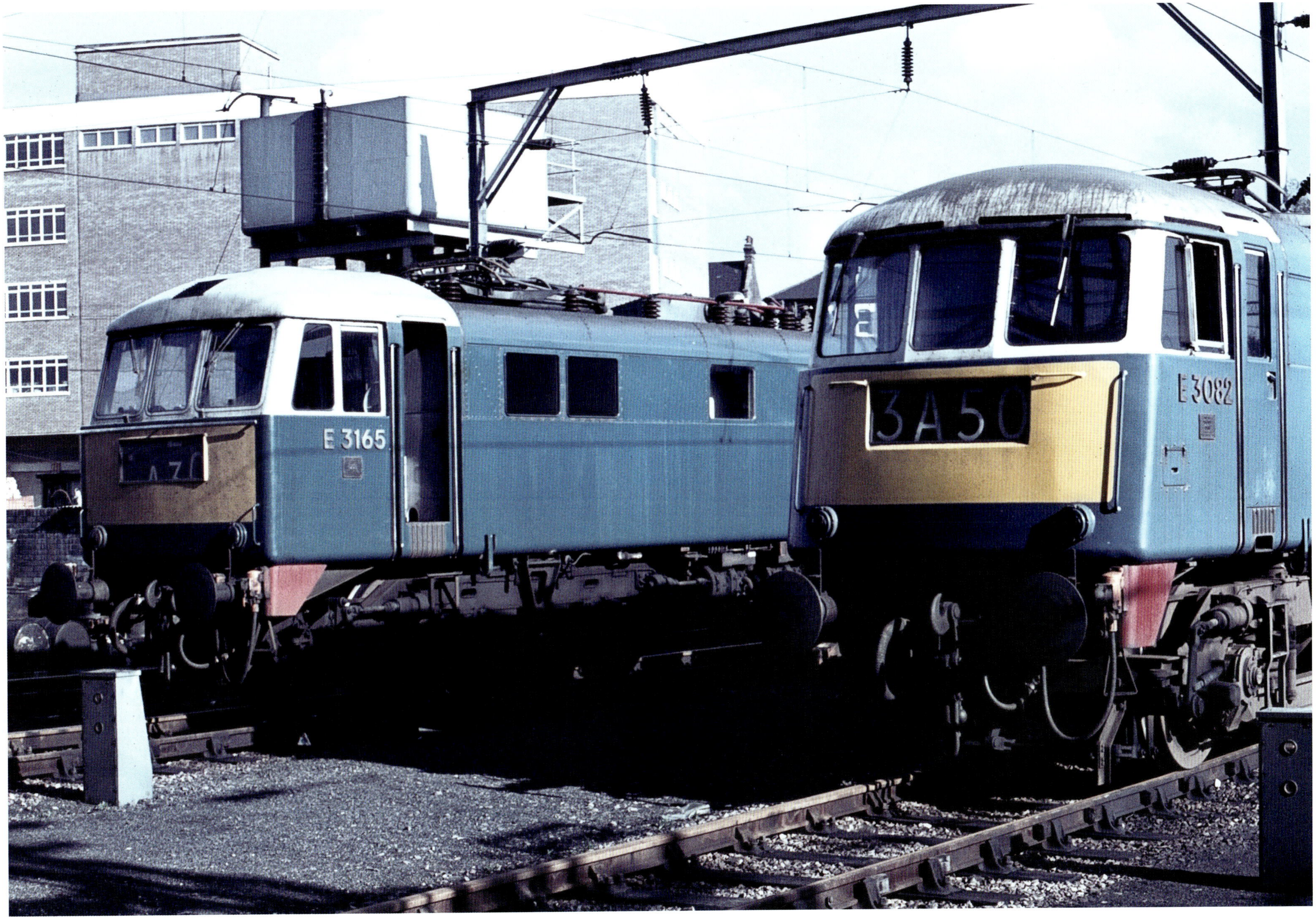
E 3165
3A50
E 3082

Two-Tone Traction

Opposite: Given time in traffic no colour scheme was going to stand the rigors of the weather, or coolant and oil leaks. On 7 September 1969, D5297 greeted our cameraman upon his entry into Crewe Diesel Depot as part of a spotting expedition from Gloucestershire. *Derek Jones*

Now repainted into the two-tone green style of the Deltics, DP2 makes a distinctive sight on shed at 34G Finsbury Park, having arrived back in this revised livery since her overhaul at Vulcan Foundry which was completed on 10 October 1965. *R.C.T.S. Archive*

In the previous picture DP2 shows the absence of any British Railways markings as she was never actually owned but was instead only on loan from English Electric. Whereas once the Deltics had been named they wore two emblems each side until repainted in to blue. The exception being D9010 which briefly managed to run in green with InterCity arrows. When D9001 St. Paddy was captured at Finsbury Park on 21 April 1962, she was just fifteen months into service and all thoughts of InterCity blue liveries for the class would another four years away. Ironically when D1105 seen here at Cardiff Canton was released brand new from Crewe Works on 9 November 1966, the first Deltic repaint into blue had already taken place at Doncaster Works upon D9002 The King's Own Yorkshire Light Infantry on 18 October, forty days previously. **Photos: Colour Rail & R.C.T.S. Archive**

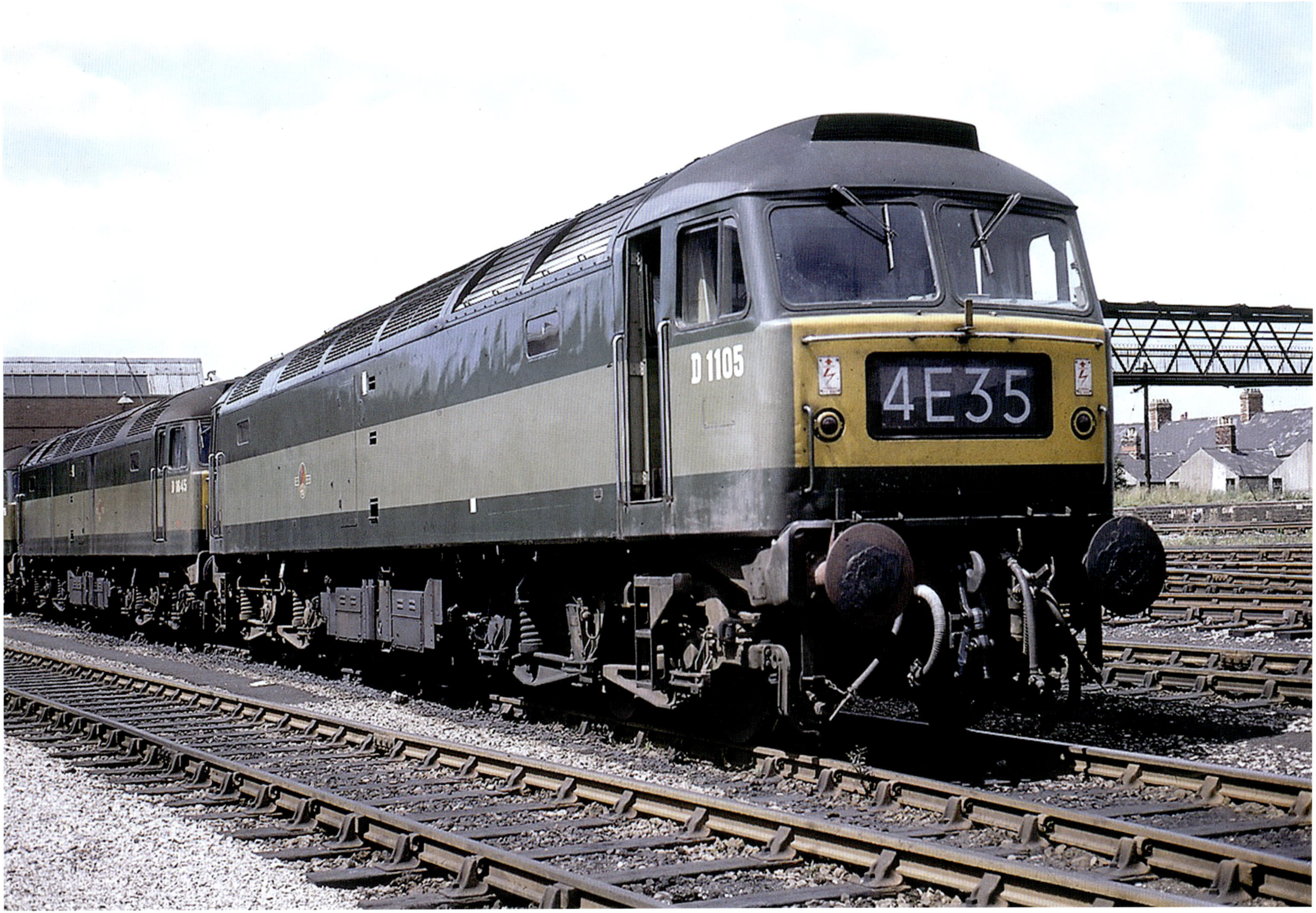
D 1105
4E35

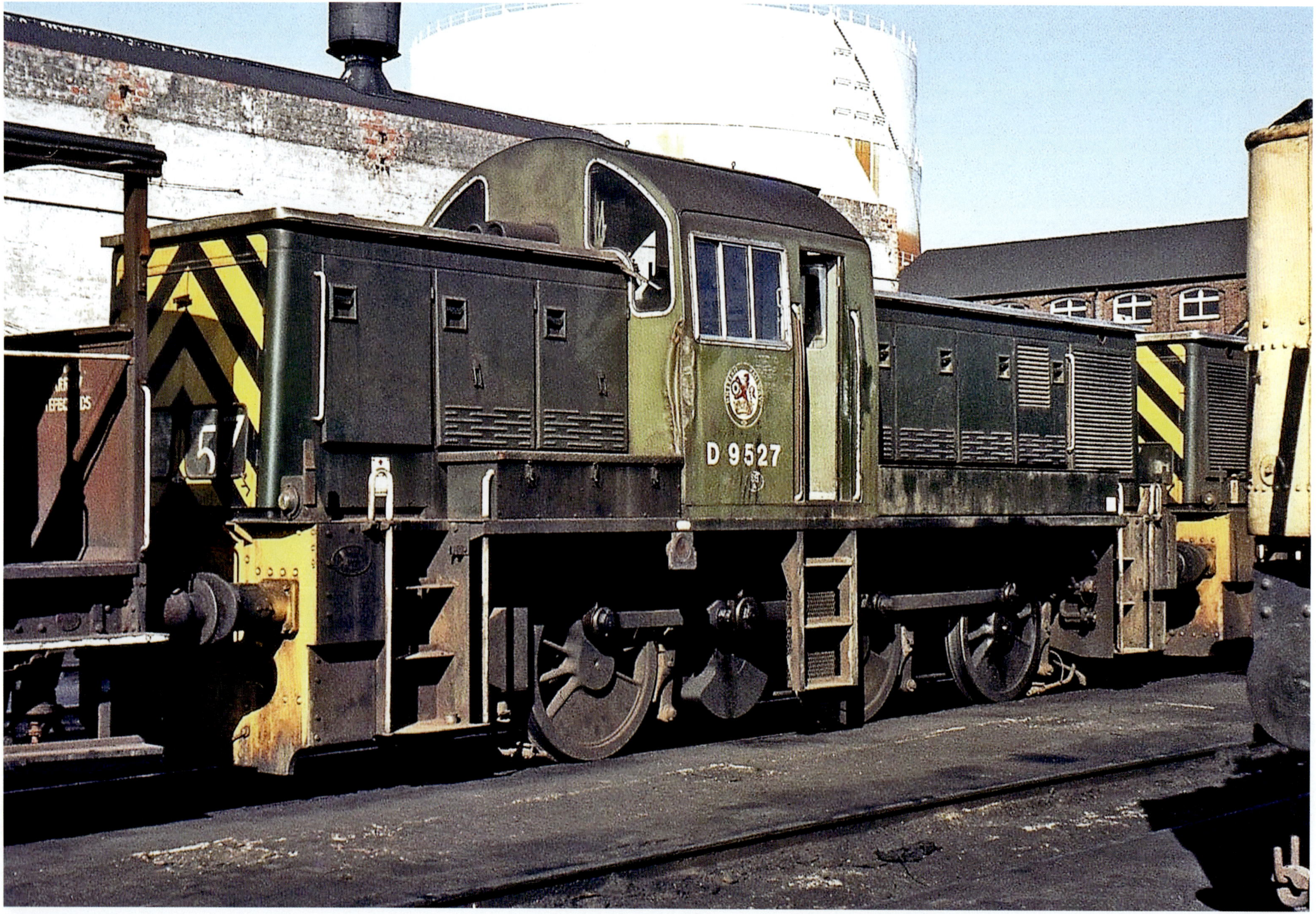
D 9527

Opposite: For sale, four and half years old, one careful owner? On 4 July 1969, D9527 was seen dumped at Gloucester Horton Road depot, she had been withdrawn officially on 22 April that year and sold to the NCB with a number of her classmates. Three others had arrived here D9502, D9514 & D9518 also on their way to Ashington Colliery. Their journey would take them via Washwood Heath and Derby arriving in Northumberland a few weeks later. *Derek Jones*

Confusion perhaps amongst the painting staff within Derby Works resulted in D5005 being returned to traffic in the style of the two-tone green livery adopted for the later versions of her more powerful sisters in Class 25, such as D5233 seen behind her. This view dates from October 1965, photographs confirm certainly that D5038, D5040 & D5053 likewise found themselves repainted the same way around this time here at Derby too. *John Ireland*

Having been part of a large production order for Type 4 locomotives awarded to Brush of Loughborough in 1962, D1743 entered traffic on 19 June 1964. Here she is on Gresford bank with an up freight on the final day of July that same year. Although she was allocated to 86A Cardiff Canton she was based out of Tyseley for crew training purposes at this time. There is still a commendable shine to the paintwork of D7060 standing outside in the sunshine within Old Oak Common's expansive depot yard on 12 February 1967. Swindon Works had already begun returning Hymeks to traffic in variations of blue livery from late November the previous year. However, this two-tone green colour scheme served D7060 through until she was withdrawn on 3 October 1971.
Photos: *Chris Forrest & Rail Online*

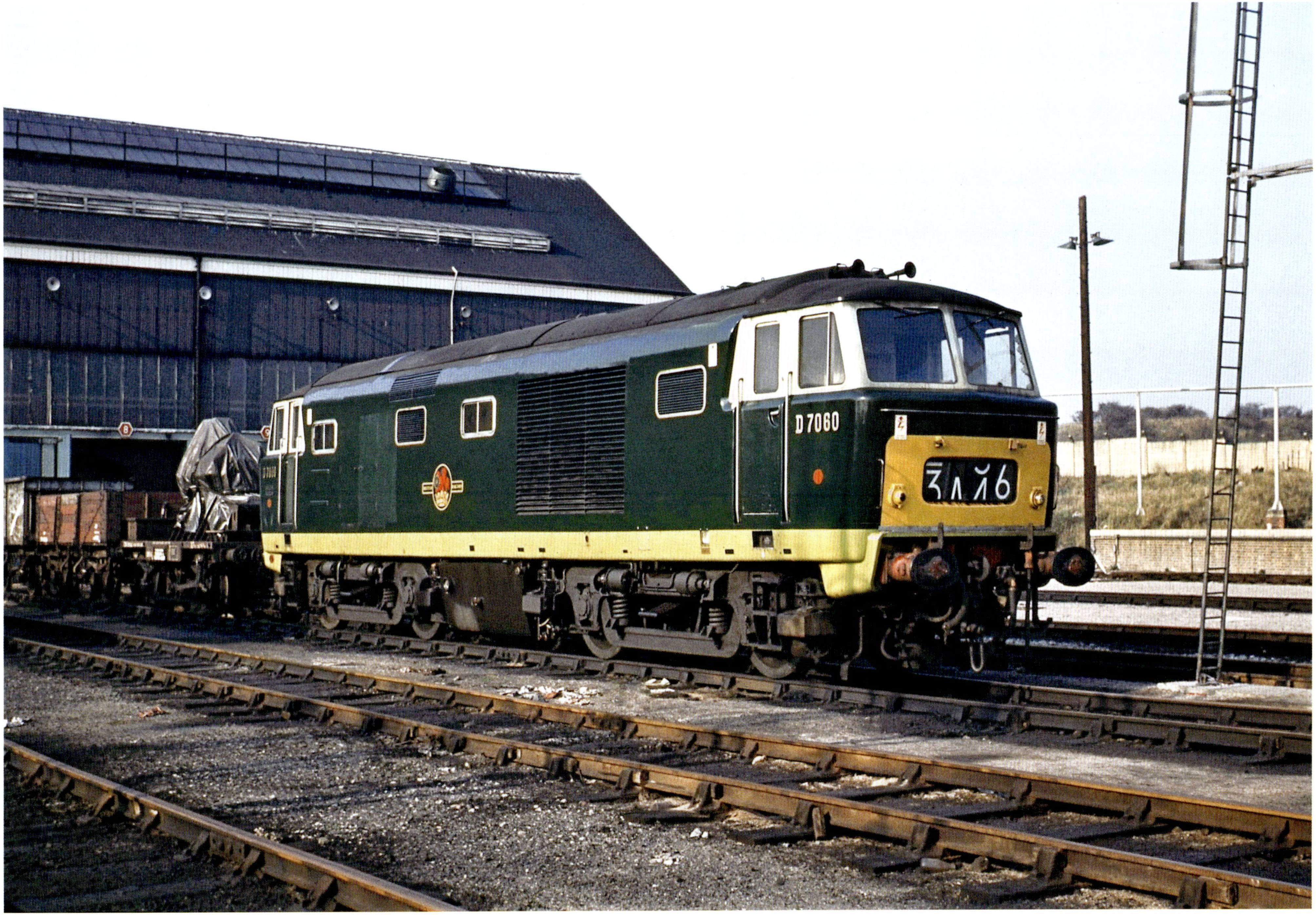
D 7060

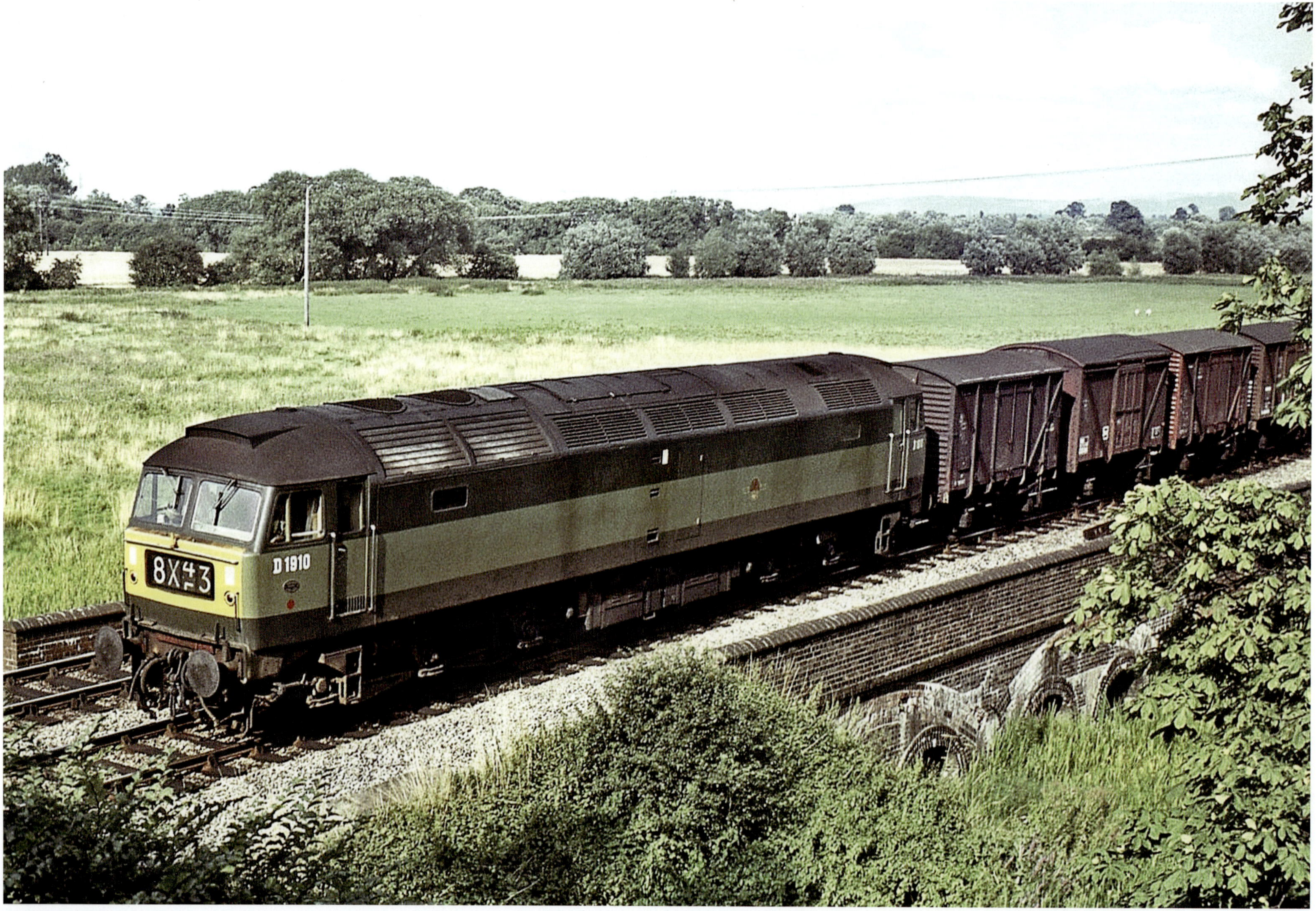
8X43
D1910

With five hundred and twelve of the class finally delivered, just ten of the Class 47s failed to enter service in their familiar two-tone green livery, these being D1733 in XP64 livery and numbers D1953 to D1961 who were in InterCity blue from Brush when new. Arriving new direct from Loughborough on 22 October 1965, D1910 joined the large allocation at 86A Cardiff Canton soon afterwards where she would remain based until May 1983. On 19 July 1969 she was seen near Over Junction with a Washwood Heath to Severn Tunnel Junction freight working. Of the ten Class 23 Baby Deltics, just one, D5909 would receive her blue livery, whereas the others all saw out their troubled lives in two-tone green. On 15 June 1969, both D5906 and D5907 who had been withdrawn the previous year languished at Doncaster Works awaiting their final disposal to George Cohen & Co. of Kettering for scrapping which took place the following month. *Photos: Derek Jones & Colour Rail*

She was destined to be the last of her class to remain in two-tone green until released from Doncaster Works, after Intermediate repairs in November 1969, in blue livery. Here D9014 The Duke of Wellington's Regiment caught the photographer's attention while stabled at York several months beforehand.
Colour Rail

As the questionably fortunate twenty examples of the fifty-eight strong NBL designed Class 21 locomotives were rebuilt with Paxman engines into Class 29, they also somehow looked refreshed externally afterwards in their new livery as demonstrated here by D6101 at Eastfield in 1968. *Dave Langham Collection*

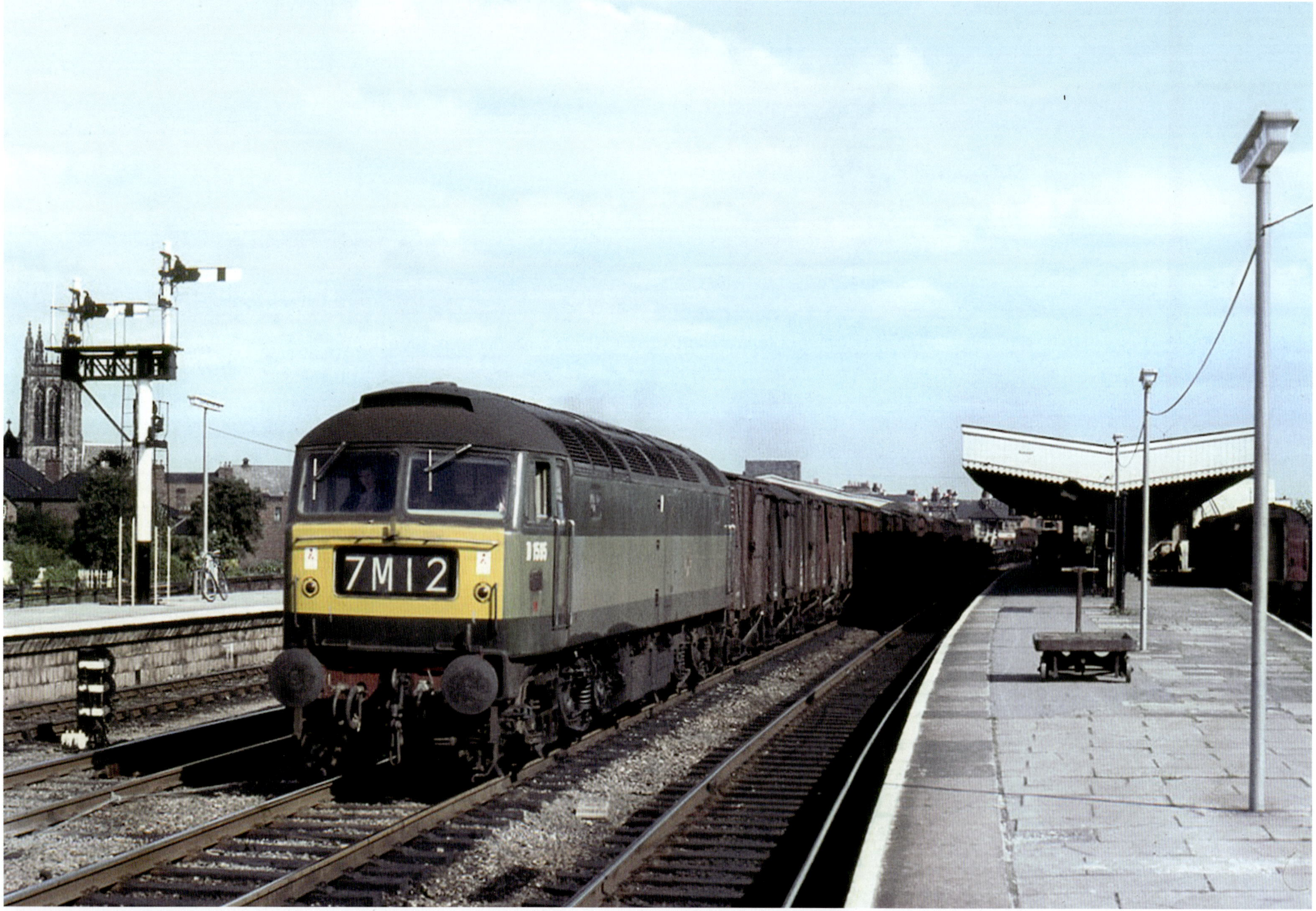
7M12

Although at the time they didn't inspire so much interest, the passage of time and the plethora of liveries that followed for Class 47s has made shots such as this with D1595 running easily through Leamington Spa station during 1966 a pleasant memory of times gone by. Likewise, during the same year on 21 October catching sight of D0280 Falcon broadside making the stop at Reading with an up service, comfortably being kept warm by her steam heating boiler. *Photos: R.C.T.S. Archive   & Colour Rail*

The painters at Derby Works in 1965 also managed to send out D5382 in this two-tone version of green seen on shed at Ayr during August 1968, similarly D5380 also gained this livery around the same time in 1965.
Colour Rail

It seems strange now that the painters at Derby didn't just repaint locomotives in the same style as they arrived in the works at this point. Except of course Derby Works was also turning out other new Type 2s such as D7503 throughout 1964 and 1965. Caught here seeing out the decade still in two-tone green albeit with the addition of a full yellow front as it graces Gloucester's Horton Road depot on 29 November 1969, drafted in to replace NBL Class 22s.
Derek Jones

In examining a range of two-tone paint schemes, we couldn't overlook the unique livery applied to HS4000 KESTREL. She certainly stood out from the crowd and was often exhibited at dedicated special events such as this Open Day at Cricklewood depot on 12 July 1969. *Anistr Railway Images*

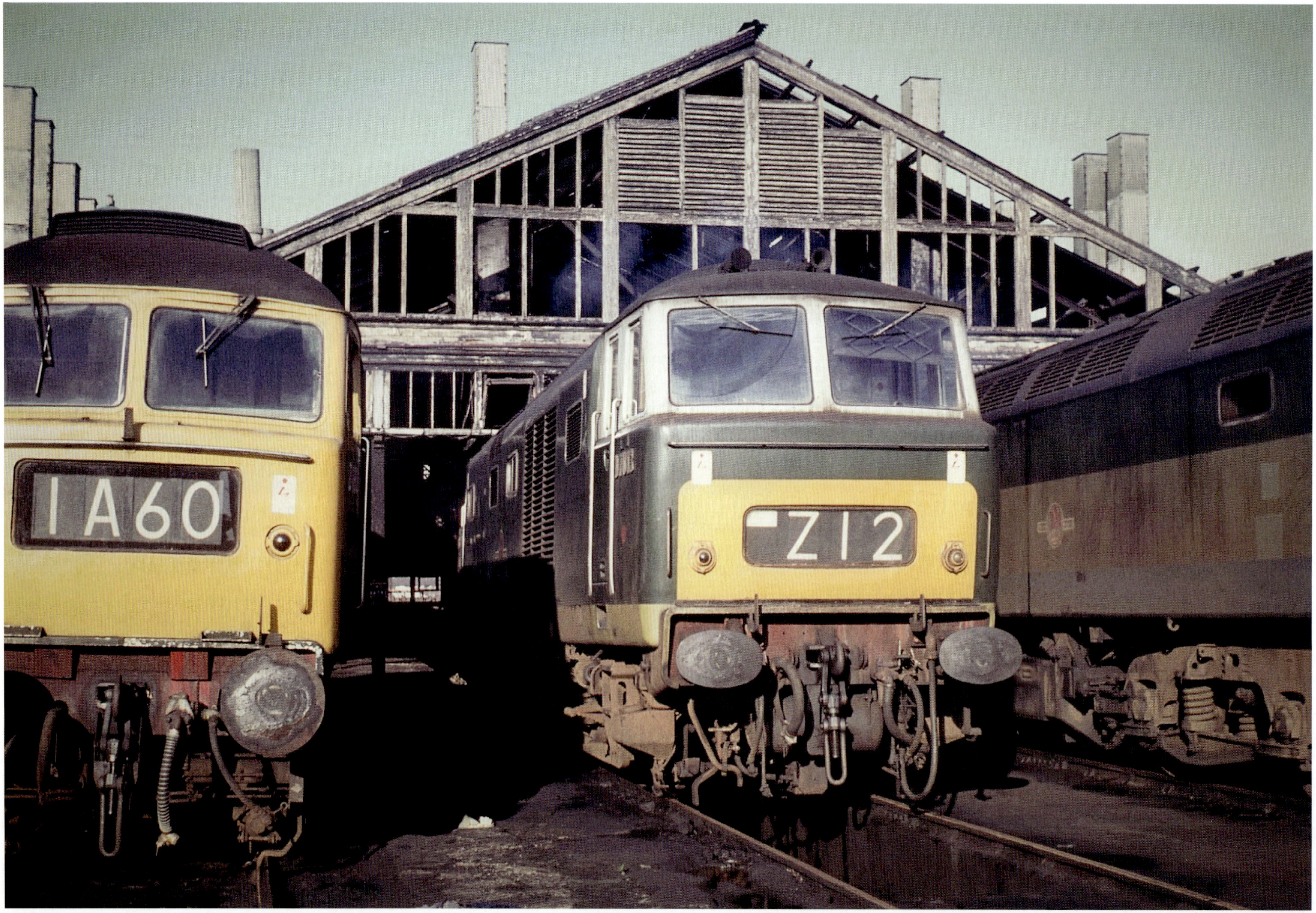
1A60
Z12

It's the early summer of 1969 just before Hymek D7013 received a full yellow end while retaining her green livery, and our cameraman has sought her out sandwiched between two Class 47s in the sunshine outside the decaying remnants of 82C Swindon shed. Truly filthy and long since neglected by any staff for cleaning, D5265 hides her filthy paintwork as she stands guard over a trio of Claytons including D8504, D8513 & D8512 among the dying gasps of steam at Kingmoor shed in Carlisle on 21 October 1967. *Photos: Rail Online & Strathwood Library Collection*

Into 1969 and both of these Class 25s D5297 and D5236 appear somewhat smarter thanks to the application of full yellow ends and a modicum of cleaning as they clatter through Derby station light engine. Likewise, the addition of further yellow paint to D1896 on her then home depot at 30A Stratford has improved her visibility too during April 1969, as she mingles with what looks like a Ford Corsair and an Austin 1100 by the staff carpark.
Photos: Dave Langham Collection & Grahame Wareham

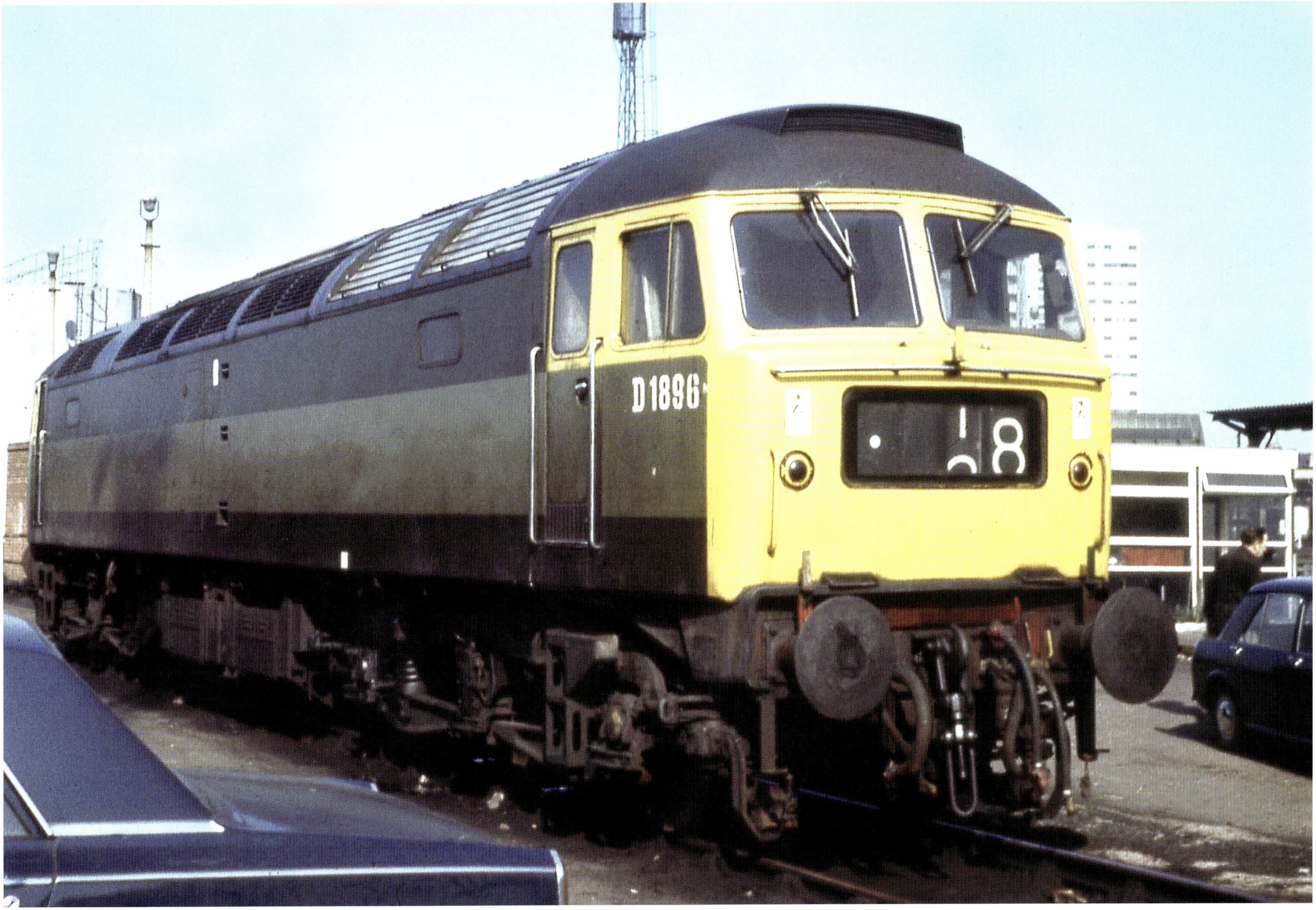
D1896

Type 1 Miscellany

With some rail borne traffic associated with the Scottish whisky distilleries Clayton Class 17, D8559 from the 64B Haymarket allocation, is just nine months into its short almost eight-year working life, and heads past the signal box at Blackford Hill on the Edinburgh suburban route controlling access to Newington Stone Yard on 13 August 1964. Whereas the working life for this English Electric Type 1, later designated as Class 20 would be much more realistic for the investment made. Introduced into service on 20 January 1960, D8031 spent its first six years on duties such as the 10.50 Ballindalloch to Craigelachie goods on 18 July 1966. It is seen here between Carron and Aberlour in the heart of Speyside's distillery country, however it will soon move from 60A Inverness to 66A Polmadie in the heart of Glasgow. Later renumbered as 20031 she was withdrawn in September 1990 and has since spent longer in the care of the Keighley & Worth Valley Railway than she did on the nationalized railway network. **Photos: R.C.T.S. Archive & Strathwood Library Collection**

Fitters can be seen providing routine servicing to an English Electric Type 1 behind D8209 in this undated shot taken at Devons Road depot most likely around the late spring of 1959. The locomotive had been delivered here when new the previous October as its first allocation from The Yorkshire Engine Co. on behalf of British Thomson Houston. Also delivered during 1958 was D8400 from North British, the first of what would become Class 16 is seen here in the yard at Temple Mills. Both classes notionally delivered 800hp in comparison to the English Electric design's 1,000hp and the Clayton's 900hp.
Both: Colour Rail

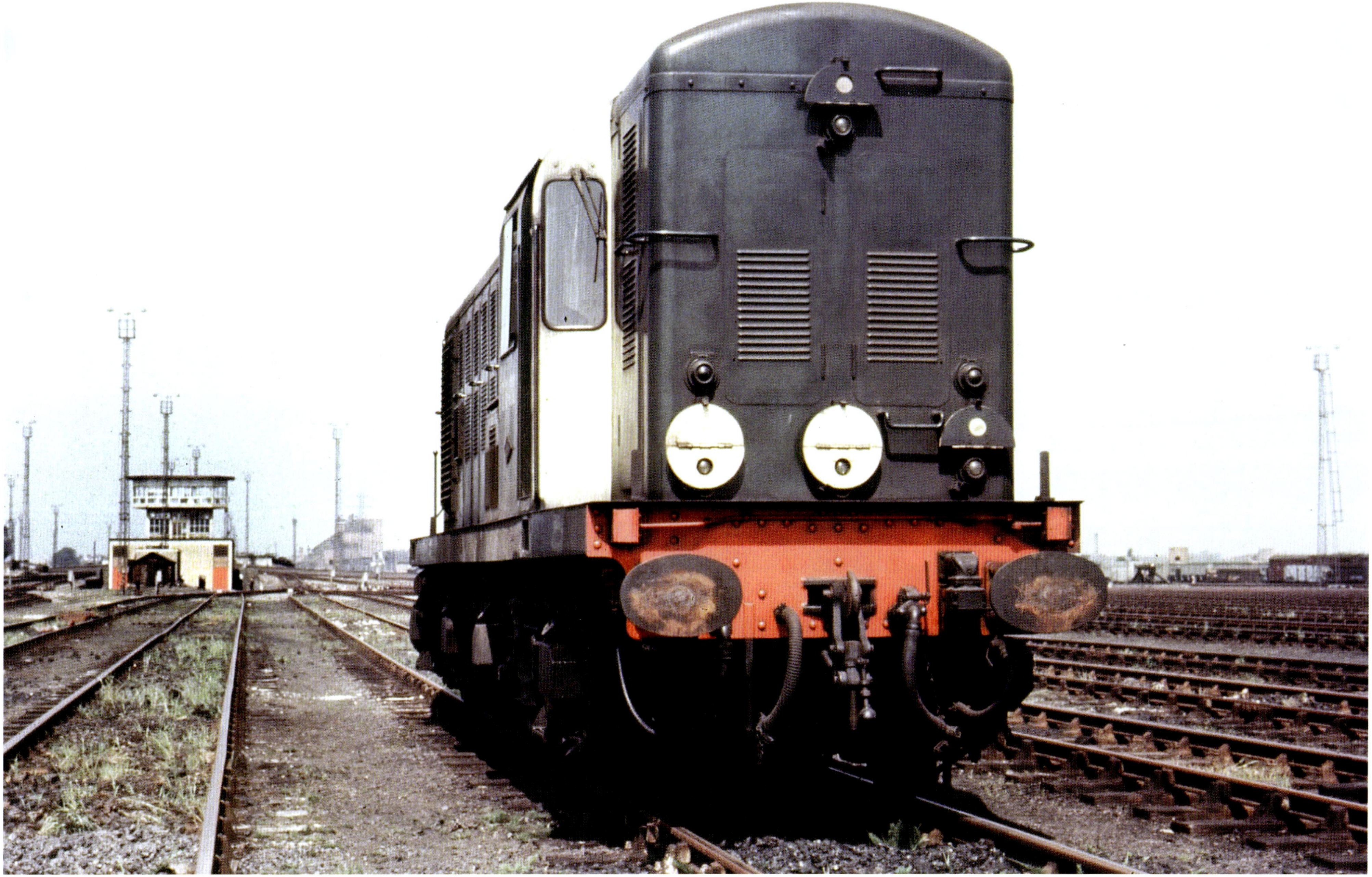

Left: With both the photographer and D8215 both fighting their way through the undergrowth at Wickham Market Junction we can see the locomotive is only working with a brake van and shows a 32B Ipswich shed plate dating this otherwise undated shot towards the earlier part of its tenure at the Suffolk depot from June 1963 until April 1966 when it was transferred to 30A Stratford. ***Colour Rail***

Right: Stratford Works' painters seem to have begun customizing their diesel locomotive's paintwork long before the 1970s. They had begun this trend on the two regular Liverpool Street steam pilots with a Class N7 and a J69 being re-painted into a style reminiscent of the former Great Eastern Railway's deep royal blue scheme in the later 1950s. What looks to be freshly applied in this 1964 view alongside Stratford Works shows a handy repeat of the locomotive's number on its ends, along with some well executed black lining around the edges of the route discs. Similarly, D8202 and D8204, D8205 & D8207 have also been seen with this style of extra numbering albeit before the application of their yellow warning panels.
Strathwood Library Collection

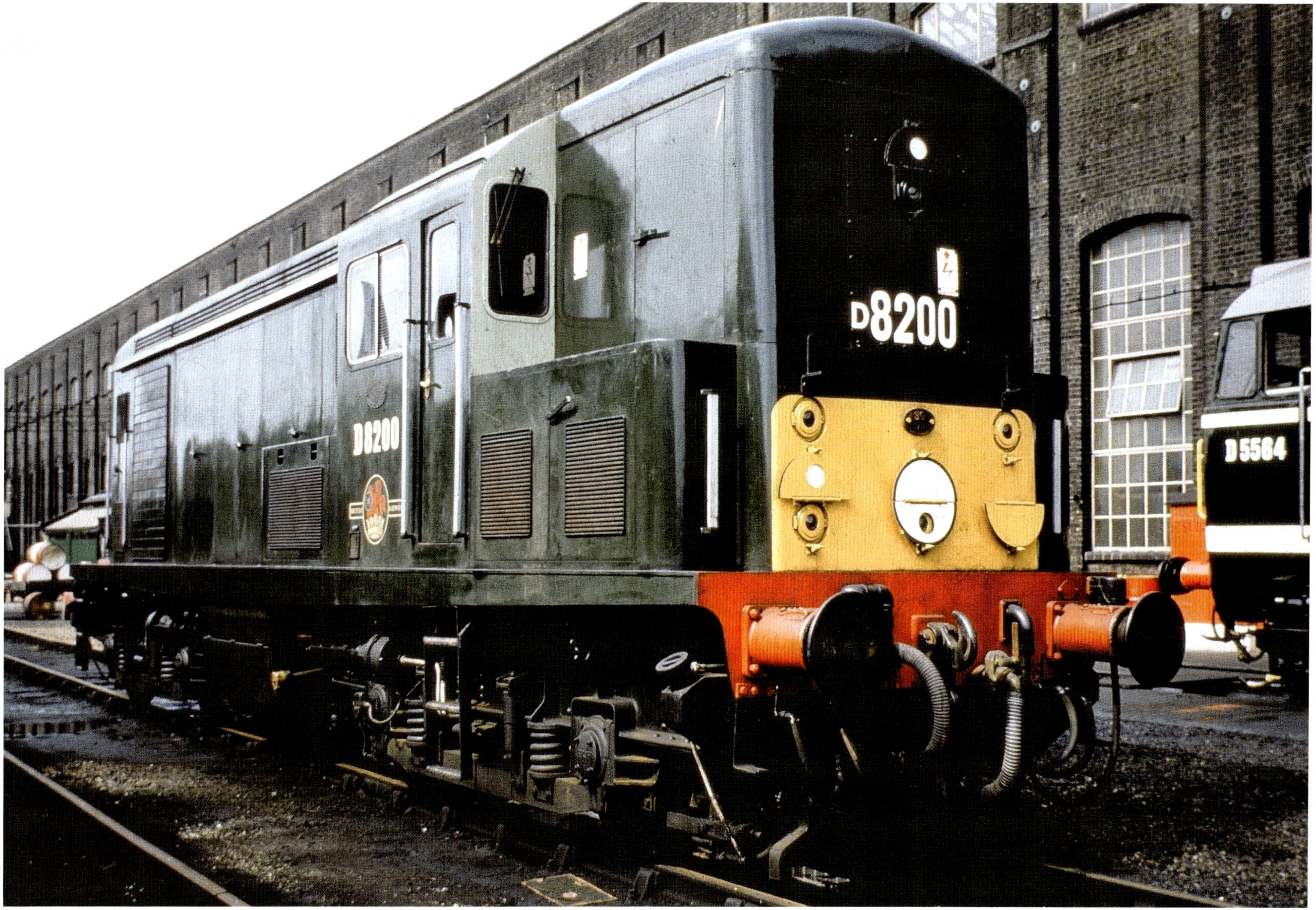
D8200
D8200
D5584

Reliability and availability of spares coupled with a rapid decline of local pick-up goods workings, which in turn brought about a surplus of Type 2 locomotives contributed towards the demise of this NBL design. The inevitable soon happened to such a small class of ten locomotives as D8404 was the first to be withdrawn with effect of 18 February 1968. Here she is discarded along with some more cast offs at Stratford shed during April 1968. The threat to the entire fleet of BTH and NBL Type 1s was dire as a number of English Electric Class 20 Type 1s could be easily found as their direct replacements, along with spare Class 31s as required. Ironically, this example D8045 which had been based at both Hornsey and here at Finsbury Park would be sent away the London area the year after this shot was taken in 1965. However other Class 20s would be drafted into serve briefly as replacements including D8031 previously seen in the far away Scottish highlands on page 113. ***Photos: John Ferneyhough & Strathwood Library Collection***

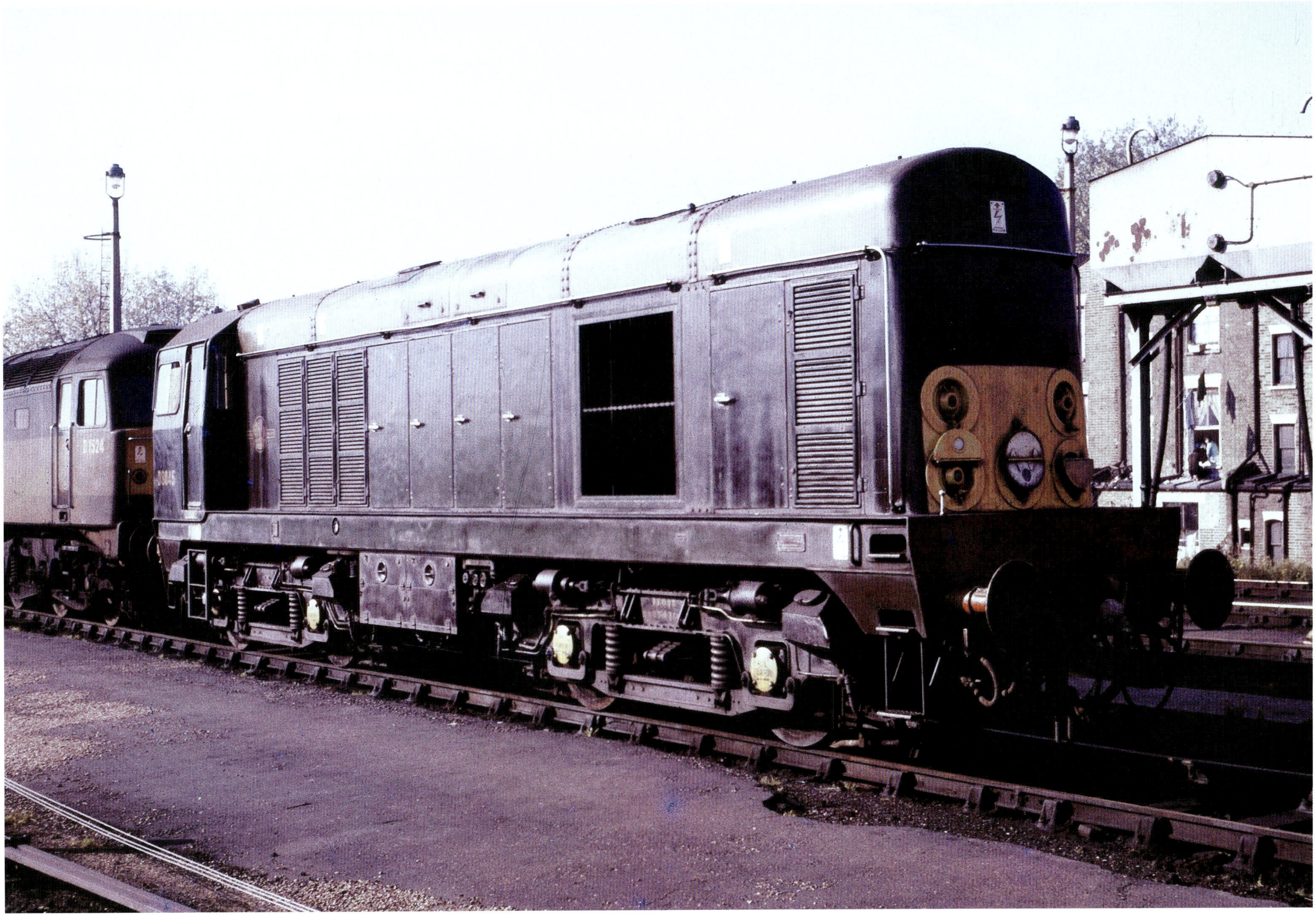

We have already cited that the Claytons had tragically short working lives, here is one that didn't even make it out of the 1960s. The story for D8585 begins with her arrival from the works of International Combustion Ltd in Derby on behalf of Clayton Ltd a subsidiary, arriving at 64B Haymarket on 1 May 1964. We see her here on a local Edinburgh grain working at Portobello East a few months later on 21 August. There may or may not have been internal problems with this example, but D8585 like so many of the class it seems often suffered several fires in service. Her last of the three she had was repaired at St. Rollox in late 1967. In October 1968, she then suffered collision damage and was set aside firstly at Haymarket, then Thornton Junction and Polmadie before being sold to the Glasgow scrap dealers J. MacWilliam at Shettleston who appear to have cut her up around the beginning of June 1969. In comparison the service life of D8215 who we see once again, this time resting in the depot yard at 31B March sometime during 1968, likewise hardly appears to be a bargain. As after trials at Derby Works in January 1960, she arrived here at March shed two months later. Further allocations went on to include Stratford, Ipswich, and a return to Stratford. Finally, her use here became less and less and she was posted as withdrawn at the close of 1970 and sent firstly to Doncaster Works for at least nine months, before being dragged to Crewe Works for final disposal after a mixed working life of barely a decade.
Photos: R.C.T.S. Archive & Strathwood Library Collection

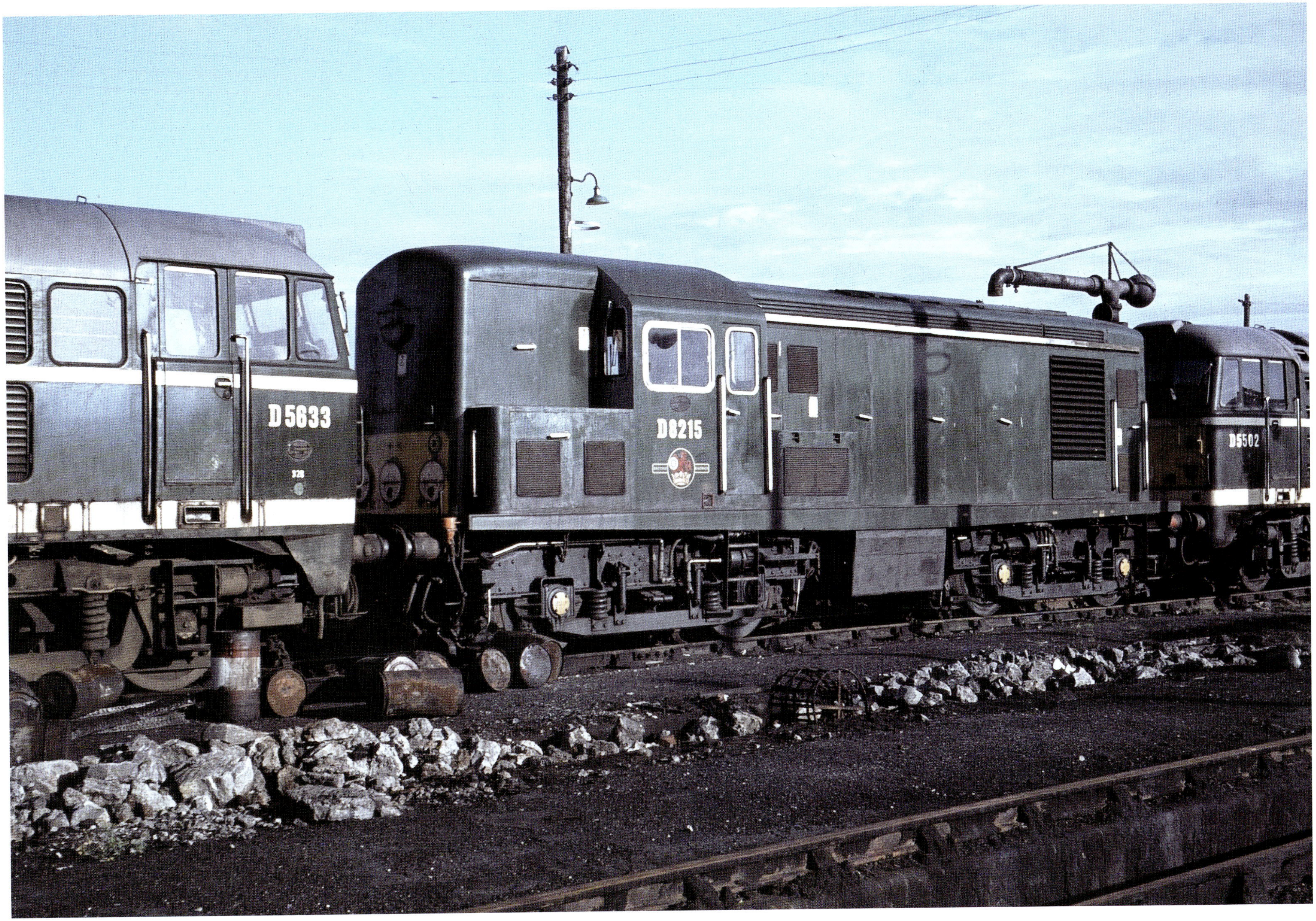
D5633
D8215
D5502

The working life on British Rail for this Class 14, D9515 seen here at Radyr soon after being built at Swindon in October 1964, would turn out to be even worse. In this case just under forty-one months, being withdrawn from Hull Dairycoates on 1 April 1968. *Strathwood Library Collection*

Raising the bar slightly on value for money perhaps and her service record would be D8610, managing seventy months of possible in-traffic use. We catch up with her on the spur at Millerhill around 1969. Already doomed before long, so it would seem, having started her career at Tinsley in December 1964, although in reality working out of Barrow Hill initially and then, officially as of April 1965. She came north to Edinburgh and Haymarket depot in May 1966, although it seems a misnomer once again as she was really working out of Aberdeen's Kittybrewster depot at first once in Scotland. A final transfer across to Glasgow and Polmadie would follow five years later, soon accompanied by withdrawal in October 1971. She then joined the hordes of her classmates for a while at Ardrossan awaiting disposal before a return to Glasgow ultimately for scrapping within the works at St. Rollox in the late summer of 1973.
Dave Langham Collection

The problems with the Claytons were really exposed early on towards the final months of 1962. Even with D8500 having been driven down to Marylebone and proudly put on display with other forms of new traction, to both officials and the public alike before that in July. The attraction of the design initially was that it had two engines, which should have meant fuel savings shutting one down when not required for shunting and to increase reliability if one failed in traffic, allowing a limp home option. The reliability with the two Paxman engines was quickly called into question however, and an embargo was placed upon any further deliveries after D8513 due to crankshaft failures. The maker's works at Tutbury, near Derby were now faced with finding the solution. Construction continued assuming improved crankshafts could be fitted to all those locomotives now awaiting delivery, thereby keeping the factory moving. By the summer of 1963 and the completion of D8521 the embargo was lifted. Before long politics and economics overtook commonsense it seems, as even though the English Electric Type 1 design was clearly proving to be much more reliable and cheaper to operate in service, a further order was placed for the already questionable Clayton design to be numbered D8588 to D8616, this was instead placed to Beyer Peacock & Co's Gorton Works, most likely in an ill-fated attempt to keep them employed. However, the final two locomotives from the first order manufactured in Tutbury were assembled using engines supplied locally from Derby by Rolls Royce, in a vain attempt to provide a final solution, which duly failed. These two locomotives could be distinguished easily with their raised bonnet cowlings as witnessed by the Rolls Royce fitted duo of D8586 and D8587 mingling with their Paxman powered stablemates here at St. Margaret's shed on 8 September 1967. Meanwhile the Gorton built batch carried on using Paxman engines and crankshafts as before, although reliability it appears improved on this second batch, but the die was cast and a large follow-on order for Type 1 machines had also been given to English Electric finally. **Colour Rail**

Although we know them as British Thomson Houston Class 15 locomotives the reality is the construction of numbers D8200 to D8209 was subcontracted out internally within what became the AEI group to The Yorkshire Engine Co. at their Sheffield Works. Furthermore, the follow-on production order involving numbers D8210 to D8243, being built by Clayton at their Derby premises. The penultimate locomotive in this final batch D8242 is seen here at Colchester around 1967. Another irony is that both the larger Paxman engines used on this design and the smaller type used on the Class 17s, were both manufactured here in Colchester. *R.C.T.S. Archive*

Two contrasting views of Type 1s both taken during 1967, firstly with the InterCity blue English Electric Class 20 D8318 at Crewe Works on 20 August, just awaiting final clearance for service having just been delivered from the nearby Vulcan Foundry. Entry into traffic would be on 10 November based out of 64B Haymarket. Whereas the dismissal from service would come in October 1989 followed by scrapping at the hands of MC Metal Processing in Glasgow over three years later. On the other hand, D9542 was a product of Swindon Works and released to traffic in two years previously in May 1965 at Cardiff Canton. With extraordinarily little work in South Wales for her after a move to Landore, a last chance of some work was grabbed, and she headed with a number of her classmates to Humberside and Hull's Dairycoates depot, where we see her on 4 March 1967. Unwanted here as well she was offered for sale a year later and snapped up by the British Steel Corporation for their expansive system at Corby in Northamptonshire just as 1969 dawned. Here she survived until she was broken up on site in August 1982. *Photos: R.C.T.S. Archive & Strathwood Library Collection*

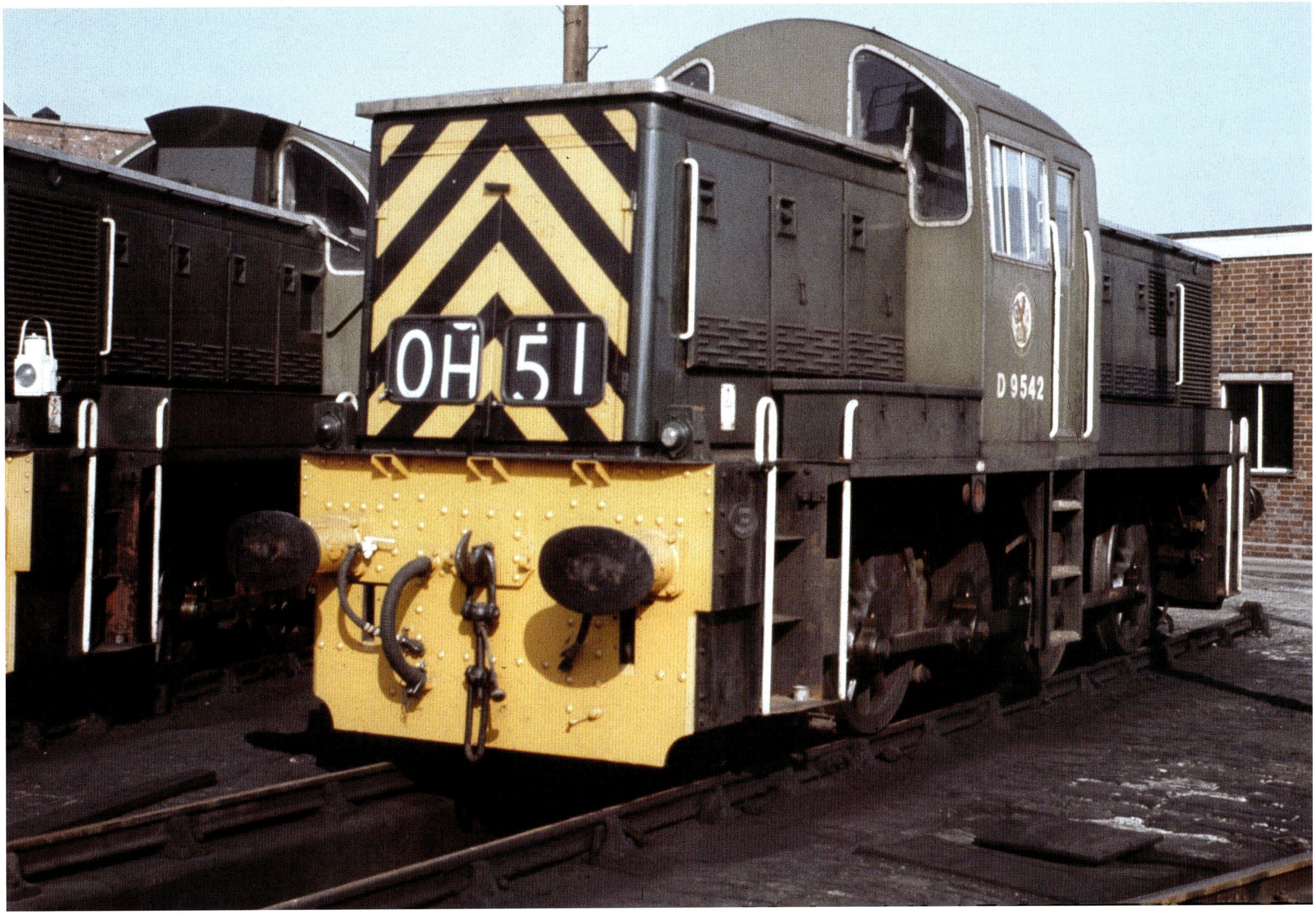
OH 51
D 9542

Two further views of Type 1s from 1967, just to show that representatives of both Classes 16 and 15 could still scrub up nicely towards the end of their days we see D8407 with her recently applied full yellow ends, snuggling up to what looks like a recently repainted green Class 15 complete with InterCity arrows in the same style as D8231 seen opposite at Hornsey, except it retains its serifs to its D prefix around the same time.
Photos: Rail Photoprints & R.C.T.S. Archive

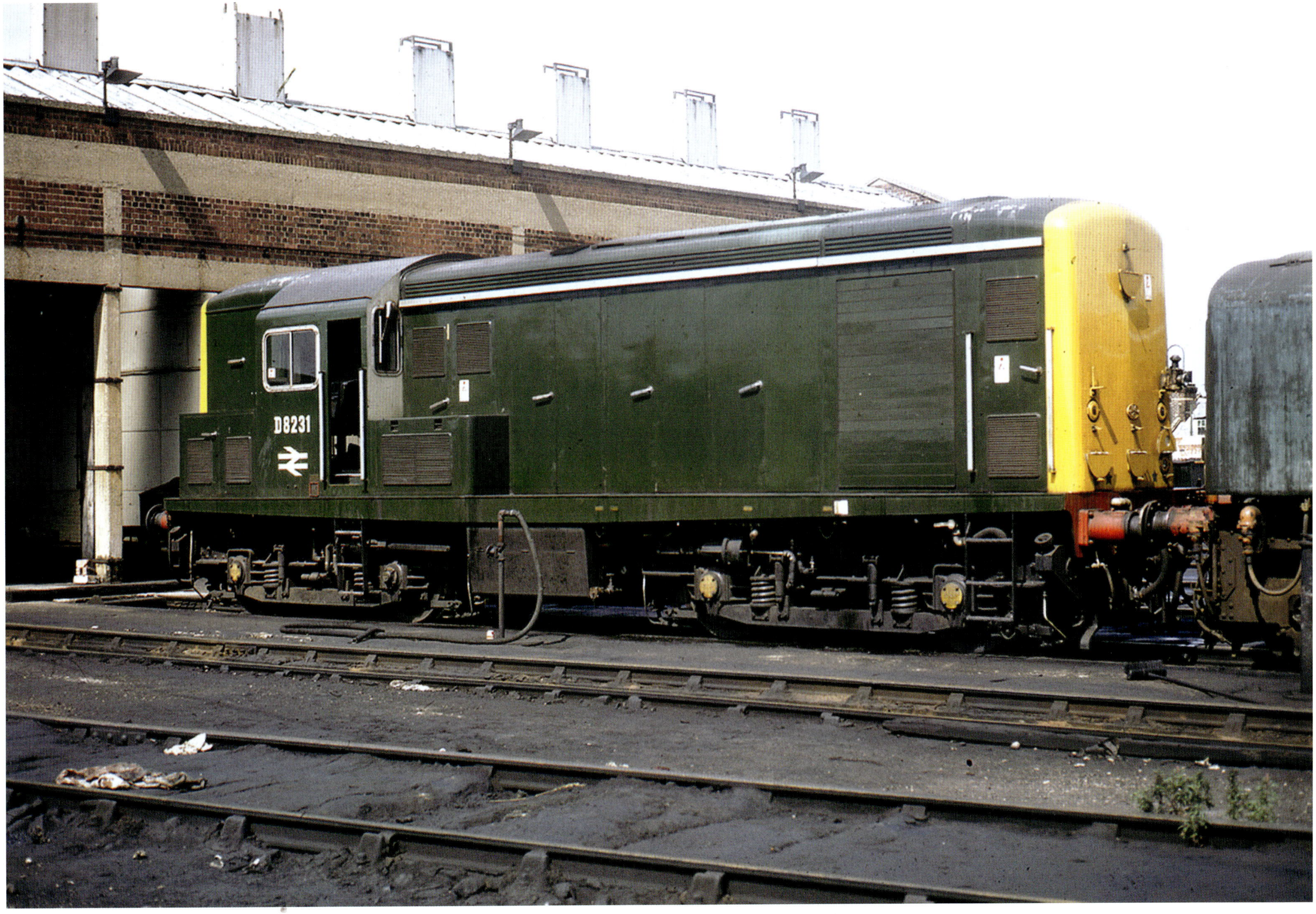
D8231

The design team at Swindon Works chose a two-tone green colour scheme for their almost central cab design, with the lighter shade being taken all the way down the cab sides. It was finished off with the later style of numbering and as was Swindon's choice for green and maroon Westerns, also on maroon Warships too during the mid-sixties was to apply the roundel version of the British Railways emblem, more readily associated with multiple units and coaching stock. The Western Region also made effective use of paint stencils to show locomotive shed codes as here on D9514 at her home shed of 86A Cardiff Canton on 23 June 1968. *Colour Rail*

Design wise the cab for the Clayton Class 17s was both central and certainly capacious. It also afforded loco crews good protection when things went wrong in collisions. The exhaust ports for each of the engines ran upwards in the middle between the forward windows, often making things both noisy and smoky. Speaking of which they were renown for not only catching fire but often leaving a pall of black smoke in their wake, especially when being thrashed as many Scottish Region drivers were famous for. The cab sides for the class were set off in this two-tone green style from new, complete with cut outs for tablet catcher apparatus, which hardly if ever seems to have been fitted. By the time of this view of D8614 at Eastfield during September 1968, full yellow ends were being applied to some of the surviving green examples, whereas a number had already been painted blue. *Grahame Wareham*

In so many ways the Swindon Class 14 design was more of a glorified shunter than a Type 1 with its coupled wheels. In terms of speed, they were not going to win any races being limited to 40mph, it would be a brave driver attempting this with a loaded goods train too, as their braking ability was questionable as well. This is the now four-year-old Teddy Bear D9514 at Pontypridd in 1968. Seen opposite having recently been given an overhaul at St. Rollox, D8583 has returned to duty in blue as we witness some light shunting going on at Haddington in September 1967. In terms of speed capabilities, these Class 17s were capable of 60mph as were both Classes 15 and 16 too, leaving the clear winner of the production Type 1 designs as the English Electric Class 20, in just about all terms including its 75mph operating capability too. *Photos: John Ferneyhough & TOPticl*

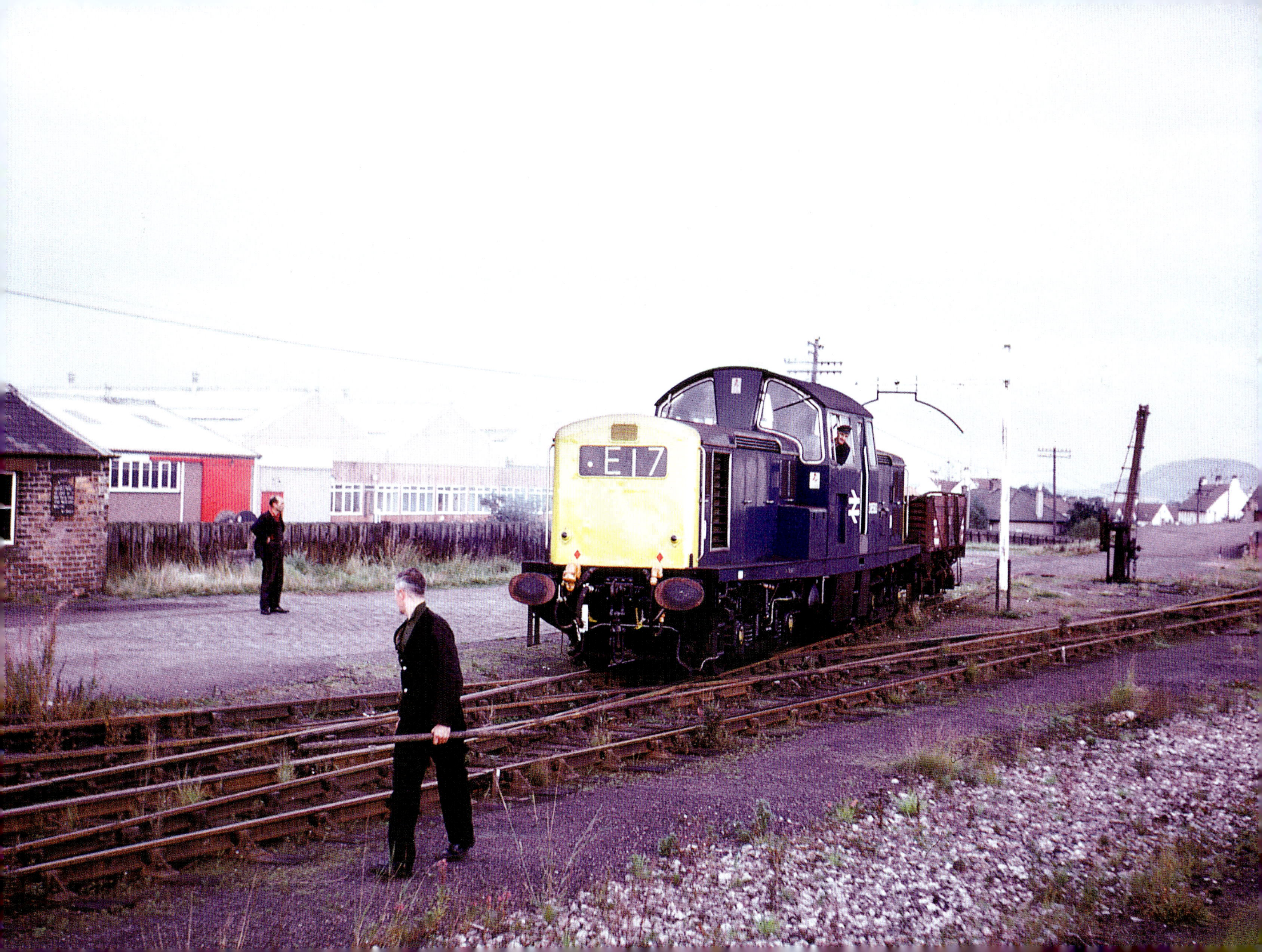
E17

What's in a Name

Eventually all twenty-two of the production Deltics would be named with some following a tradition begun in the early days of the LNER to acknowledge winning racehorses, most especially those associated with famous races and racecourses served by their lines. Thus, we have D9009 coming on fast at Prestonpans some time in 1962, having gained the name Alycidon in a ceremony at Doncaster station on 21 July the previous year. The name recalls a racehorse owned by the 17th Earl of Derby that went on to win The Ascot Gold Cup, Goodwood Cup, Corporation Stakes, and the Doncaster Cup. With such prowess the stallion went on to sire another racehorse whose name was used on D9003 Meld. Eight of the class would gain racehorse names whereas the remainder would ultimately be named to honour army regiments, such as D9006 seen at Haymarket in 1965 bearing the nameplate The Fife & Forfar Yeomanry, complete with their proud badge linking them with the Scottish Horse. Their formation was in 1793 enjoying action in the Second Boer War, followed by both world wars. In their later years as an armored tank regiment, they were based at Cupar in Fife until disbanded in 1975. Appropriately D9009 was named at the town's station on 5 December 1964. **Photos: Strathwood Library Collection & Colour Rail**

135

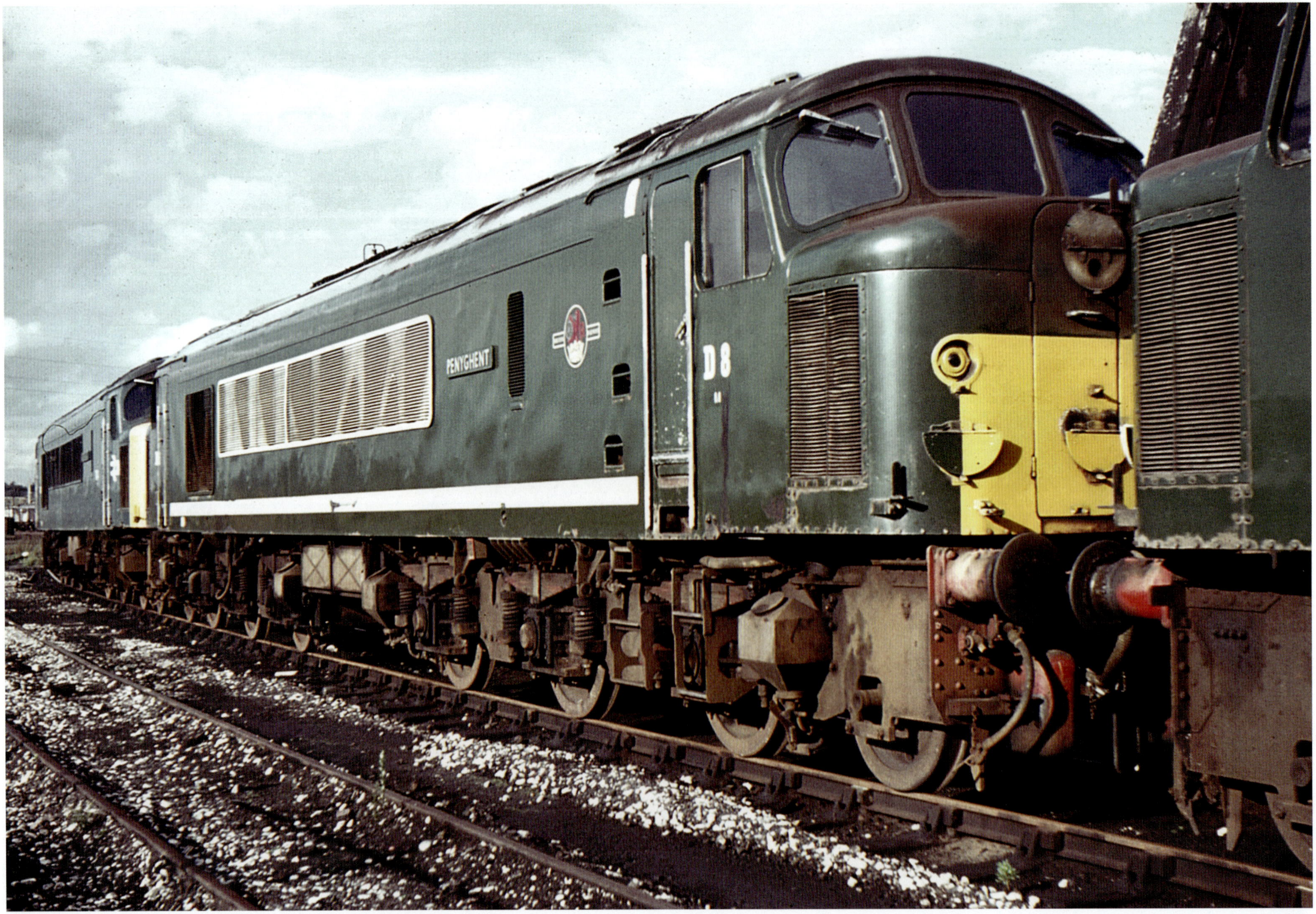
PENYGHENT
D8

The naming theme given to the first ten of the Derby Works built, and Sulzer powered 1Co-Co1s upon their introduction in 1959 was after British mountains. As a result, the name Peaks, stuck as the nickname for the remaining one-hundred-and-eighty-three locomotives that followed. Even though not all would be named, nor would they be after Peaks anymore either. Here we see D8 Penyghent in the weekend line up as usual at Toton during 1968. Three locomotives enjoyed names drawn from the high peaks of fells in the Yorkshire Dales with Penyghent at 2,277 feet being the lowest of those chosen, the other two used would be D6 with Whernside and D7 taking the name of Ingleborough. Twenty-seven of the later more powerful locomotives now colloquially known as Peaks such as D100 gained regimental names instead, in this case Sherwood Forester, who were a line infantry regiment raised within Derbyshire and Nottinghamshire. D100 was awarded the name in a ceremony at Derby Midland station on 23 September 1961, we catch sight of the locomotive appropriately in the lines adjoining Derby Works and station a few years later in the mid-sixties. ***Photos: Dave Langham Collection & R.C.T.S. Archive***

The driver of 27003 Diana looks relaxed and comfortable from the warmth of his cab on what we can assume was otherwise, a pretty unfriendly wet evening here at Sheffield Victoria in March 1966. The names of all seven of these Co-Co electrics were derived from a mix of Greek and Roman goddesses, in this instance Diana who has been described variously as the goddess of the Moon, child birth and the hunt within legends. On the other hand, the twelve production Bo-Bo electrics on the Woodhead route that were also given names, conversely saw them drawn from the mythological gods instead. The name of Hector who was a prince of Troy and considered as their greatest warrior of the Greeks in their war with the Trojans was given to 26048 and was applied at Gorton Works in March 1960 and was only carried until the late sixties it seems as witnessed here on 3 March 1968 during a visit to Crewe Works.
Photos: Colour Rail & The KDH Archive

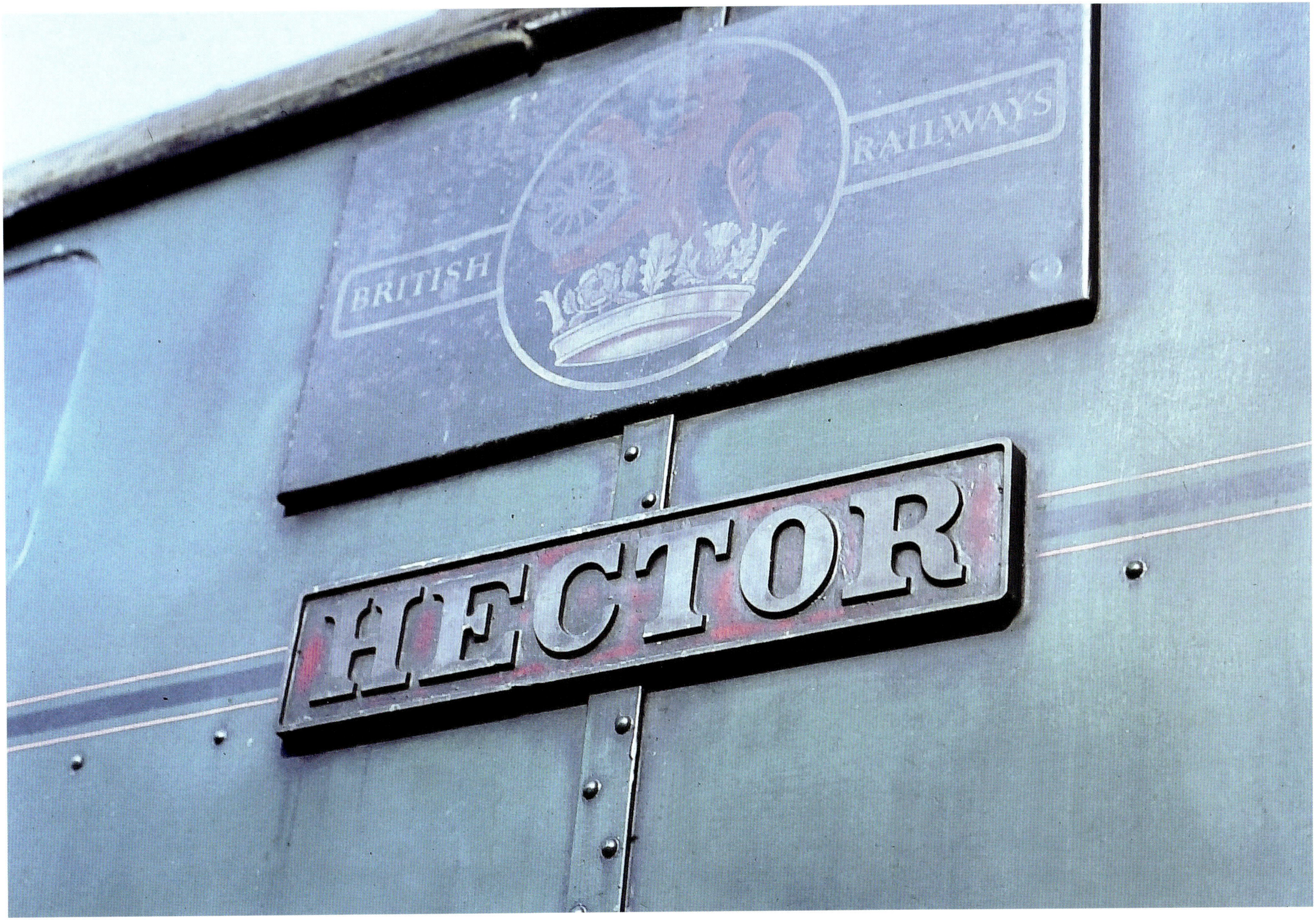
BRITISH
RAILWAYS
HECTOR

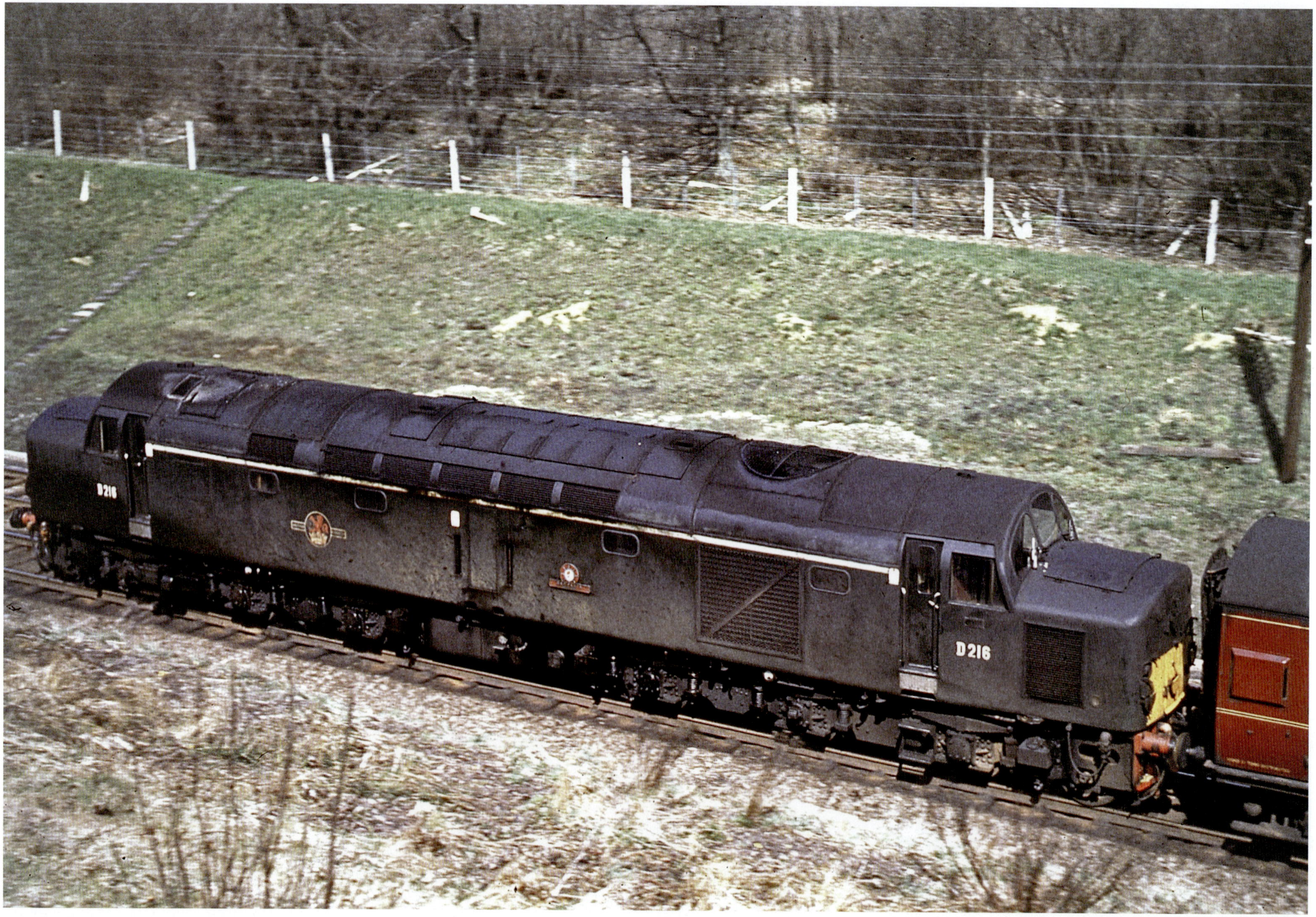
D216
D216

Left: The choice of name for D223 as Lancastria is a much more poignant one associated with Liverpool. As being a British registered ocean liner the Lancastria was requisitioned by the government during the Second World War and was sunk on 17 June 1940 during Operation Aerial. Having received an emergency order to evacuate British nationals and troops from France as a prelude to Dunkirk. The ship was loaded well in excess of its capacity of 1,300 passengers, and modern estimates suggest that between 4,000 and 7,000 people onboard died during the sinking off the French coast — now regarded as the largest single-ship loss of life in British maritime history.
Strathwood Library Collection

Opposite: The names chosen by the London Midland Region to name twenty-five of their allocation of English Electric 1Co-Co1 Types 4s reflects their historic involvement with the port of Liverpool and some of the great ocean liners of the past. For example, D216 was named as Campania which was the largest and fastest passenger liner afloat briefly when she entered service in 1893 for Cunard. She crossed the Atlantic in less than six days, and on her second voyage the same year, she also won the prestigious Blue Riband.
Colour Rail

Right: The attractive style of design chosen incorporated a ship's wheel around the pennant of the respective shipping line along with their name beneath the name of the commemorated vessel. The name as Empress of Canada was worn by D232 after she was named in Derby Works on 17 March 1961, twenty-two months after the locomotive had entered service. When D232 was named the latest liner of several predecessors to carry this name was only about to begin its first year of service regularly traversing the transatlantic route between Liverpool and Canada through the sixties. *The KDH Archive*

Staying with a maritime theme the Western Region had begun naming the first five of its new diesel-hydraulic Co-Co locomotives after Royal Navy Warships. This theme was followed on by the later deliveries of both Swindon and North British built Bo-Bo types too. That is after the gratification given to D800 as Sir Brian Robertson at the time of naming on 3 June 1958, who had been the Chairman of the British Transport Commission since 1953. It should also be mentioned this gentleman enjoyed a very impressive military background during the Second World War, more of this shortly. Working through both Classes 42 and 43 the locomotive names were chosen in alphabetic order after D801 at Vanguard and D802 as Formidable starting with D803 as Albion and ending with D870 as Zulu, with the name of Despatch previously allocated to D812 giving way to become Royal Naval Reserve 1859-1959. Thus, we see D824 when brand new named as Highflyer in July 1960. HMS Highflyer was the lead ship in her own class of cruisers dating from the 1890s. Although she had been reduced to the role of a training ship by the outbreak of World War One, she still had successes including intercepting a Dutch ship carrying German troops and gold. She then sank the German armed cruiser SMS Kaiser Wilhelm der Grosse off the coast of the Spanish Sahara, before spending most of the rest of the war on convoy escort duties before being sold for scrap in 1921. For D802 introduced in December 1958 she was given her name to recall HMS Formidable the Illustrious Class aircraft carrier that served during the Second World War who fought with distinction in not only the Home Fleet, but also in campaigns in the Mediterranean and the Indian Ocean too. She was also involved in several attacks on the German battleship Tirpitz. Formidable ended the war in the Pacific against Japanese targets before being used to repatriate liberated Allied prisoners of war and soldiers after the Japanese surrender. For those with an eye for detail notice how the nameplate fixings differ between the two locomotives. *Both: Colour Rail*

BRITISH RAILWAYS

FORMIDABLE
WARSHIP CLASS

The twenty-fifth of the Warships to be repainted into maroon and released by Swindon Works was D838 Rapid in late June 1966 when this shot was taken. HMS Rapid was a Royal Navy R Class destroyer being recognized for seeing service during the Second World War in both the Atlantic and Indian Oceans. In August 1945 she was to be prepared for the planned landings on Malaya as part of Operation Zipper, which were then cancelled upon the Japanese surrender after the dropping of atomic bombs. *Colour Rail*

We have already mentioned D800 named as Sir Brian Robertson, but what of the man himself. During the Second World War he played important roles in two African campaigns and in Italy. But his service honours first begun in World War One, winning a Military Cross and Distinguished Service Order. His skills to organize matters were first recognized by Field Marshall Montgomery who considered his abilities as the best in the British Army. If his full honours were to have been recognized by the British Transport Commission when the nameplates were applied they would have been considerably longer in 1958 as Sir Brian Robertson GCB GBE KCMG KCVO DSO MC DL. *Colour Rail Rail*

The name of Conquest was awarded to D603 in November 1958 upon delivery from the North British Locomotive Company in Glasgow. HMS Conquest was commissioned into service in June 1915 and assigned to help guard the North Sea and the English Channel from German attacks. Her crew fought bravely on 25 April 1916 helping to repel a German naval bombardment to the towns of Great Yarmouth and Lowestoft with the loss of twenty-five of her attachment. *Rail Photoprints*

Evidence suggests one idea of naming proposed for the Swindon and Crewe built Co-Co hydraulics later classified as Class 52 and forever known to us as Westerns, was instead to reflect locations served by the Western Region. After all Swindon had commemorated many Counties, Castles, Halls, Granges, and Manors previously within or around their domain. The first name put forward for D1000 is reported as being Cheddar Gorge. Officials agreed finally to an extensive list of names preceded by the reference Western. The name chosen for D1059 would be as Western Empire, the names using Emperor and Empress having been used upon D1036 and D1037. The authorities at Swindon had always been keen for naming locomotives, so proposals were also put forward to name some of the region's Brush Type 4s. Themes included reflecting upon their own illustrious names and trends from the broad-gauge era. In this way D1666 seen here at Exeter St. Davids on 23 June 1967 became Odin. **Photos: Colour Rail & Exe Rail**

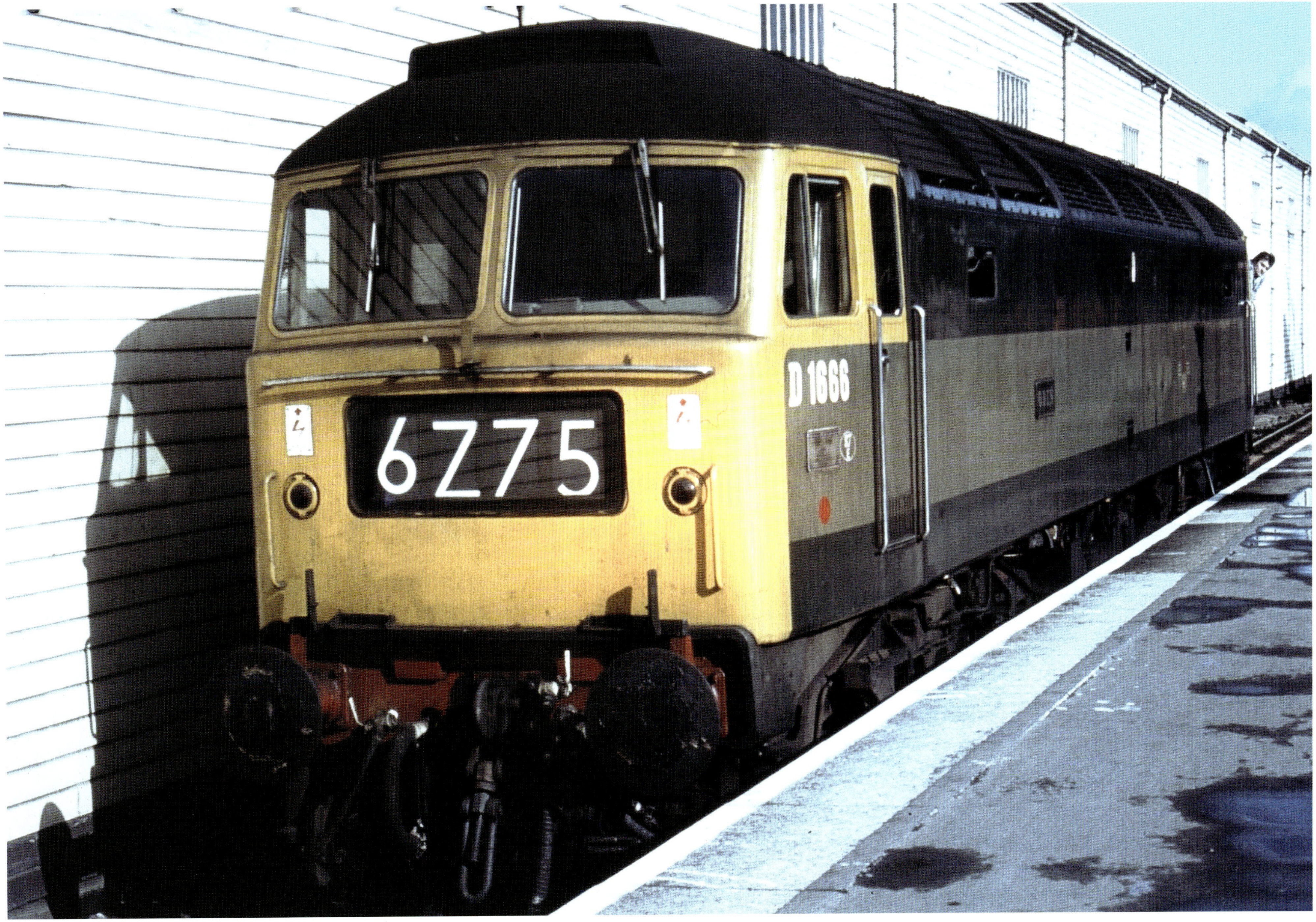
6Z75
D 1666

When the seventeen names were bestowed upon some of the Western Region's Brush Type 4s in the mid-sixties they really stood out from the rest, unlike the mass naming's that followed in later years. In this spread we can recall D1662 Isambard Kingdom Brunel at Cardiff Canton in the summer of 1965 having been named on 20 March the same year. While D1669 Python passes a deserted Reading yard in 1969, and D1672 Colossus greets visitors to Old Oak Common in 1967. *Photos: Bob Treacher & TOPticl*

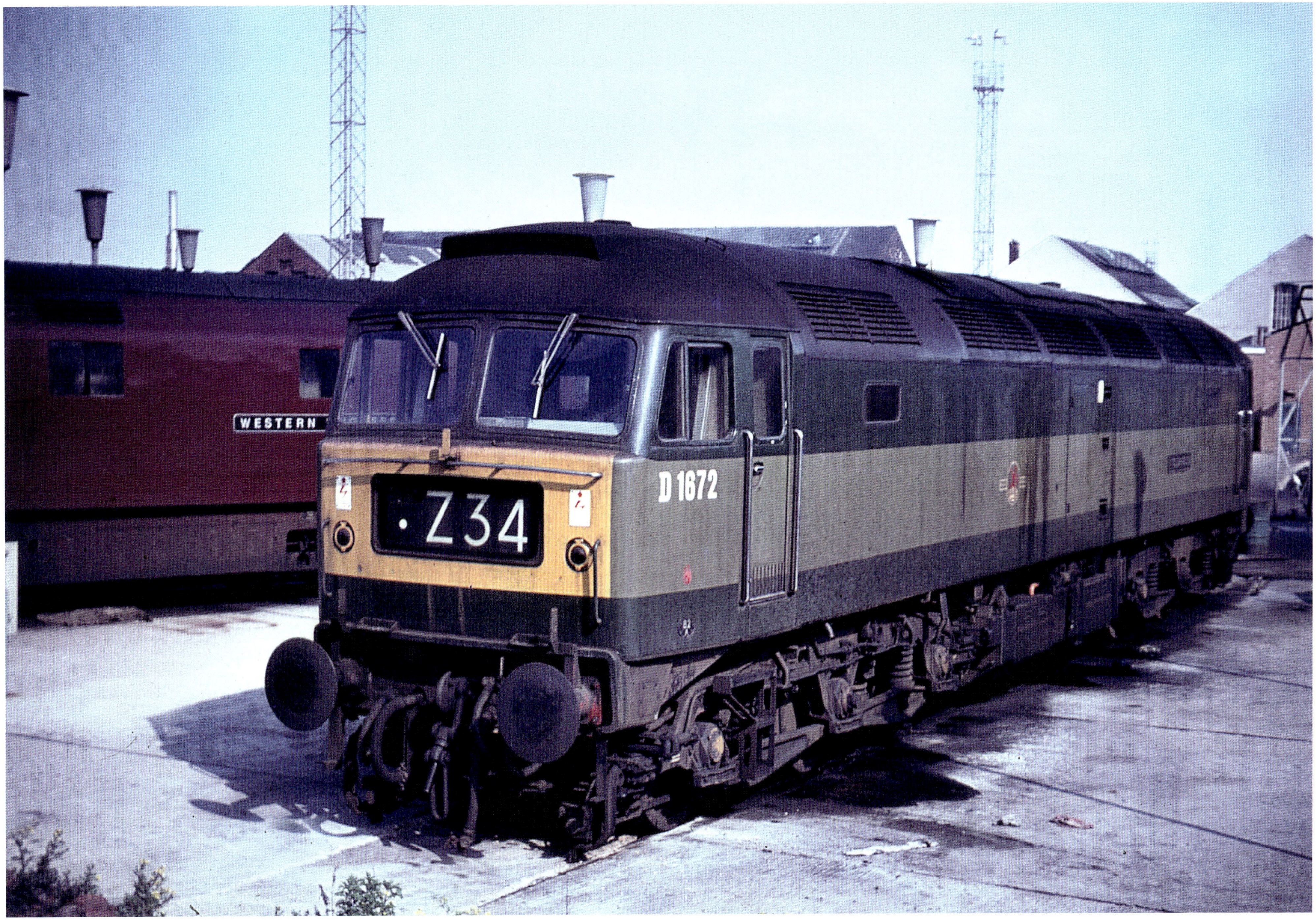
WESTERN
D 1672
Z34

Works Visits

Works visits always seemed to be both fascinating and rewarding for our notebooks too back in the sixties, as we made our way around usually as part of organized groups or open days rather than bunking, as was more the norm at depots and stabling points. The very much dismantled D6319 and D7070 form the center of attraction in this undated view at Swindon Works thought to be around 1966. An earlier visit in the summer of 1962 to Eastleigh brings us a recently repainted E5011 in the now plain green livery adopted by the Southern Region over the previously lined version as supplied by Doncaster Works when it was new in 1959. *Both: Colour Rail*

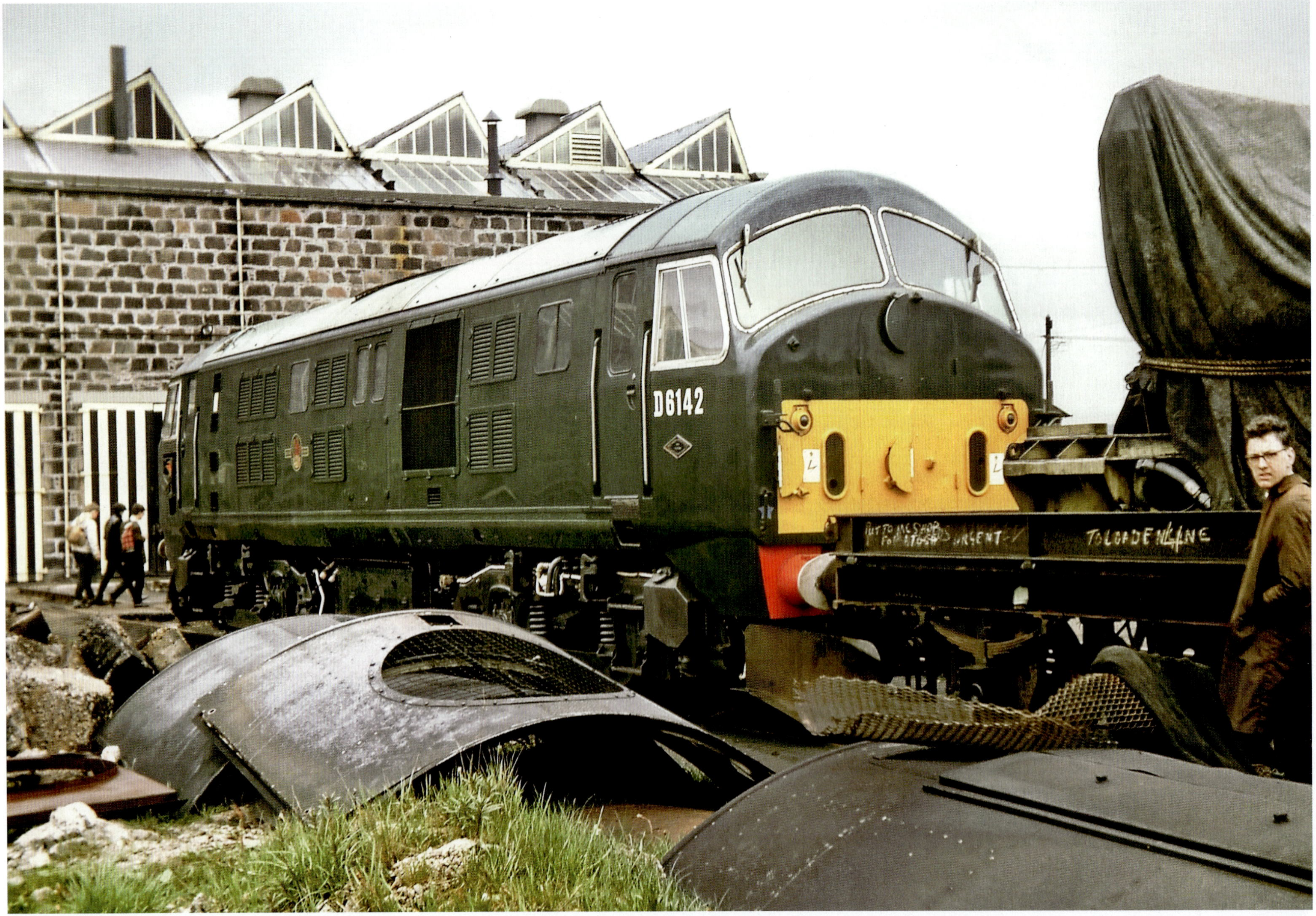
D6142

As steam gave way to diesel during the mid-sixties in Scotland major repairs on the new traction were still undertaken within the former Great North of Scotland Railway's workshops at Inverurie, as here in May 1966 on this North British Class 21. Alternatively, the former Caledonian Railway's workshops at St. Rollox would also attend to their needs as on this now freshly rebuilt and newly returned with Paxman engines as a Class 29 retaining the number D6102 in July the same year. Sadly, the final locomotives to be overhauled at Inverurie left in 1969 as the works closed completely.
Gordon Edgar Collection/Rail Photoprints & TOPticl

Freshly repainted and sparkling in the sunshine at Stratford having just received its new yellow warning panel as part of its overhaul now in its third year of traffic we see D5519. Meanwhile the workshop doors are opening to allow Class J69/1 68499 to shove a sickly British Thomson Houston Type 1 Bo-Bo inside to this former Great Eastern Railway works for some more serious attention from the fitters. *Colour Rail*

One Sulzer powered Bo-Bo D5163 from nearby 51L Thornaby has been returned here to the former North Eastern Railway's Darlington Works on 23 March 1963 for attention as fellow spotters make their way around noting down the numbers of not only the dying steam fleet but also the other new Sulzer later designated as Class 25s still being built here. Three years later and the works was being rundown completely towards its full closure. *Colour Rail*

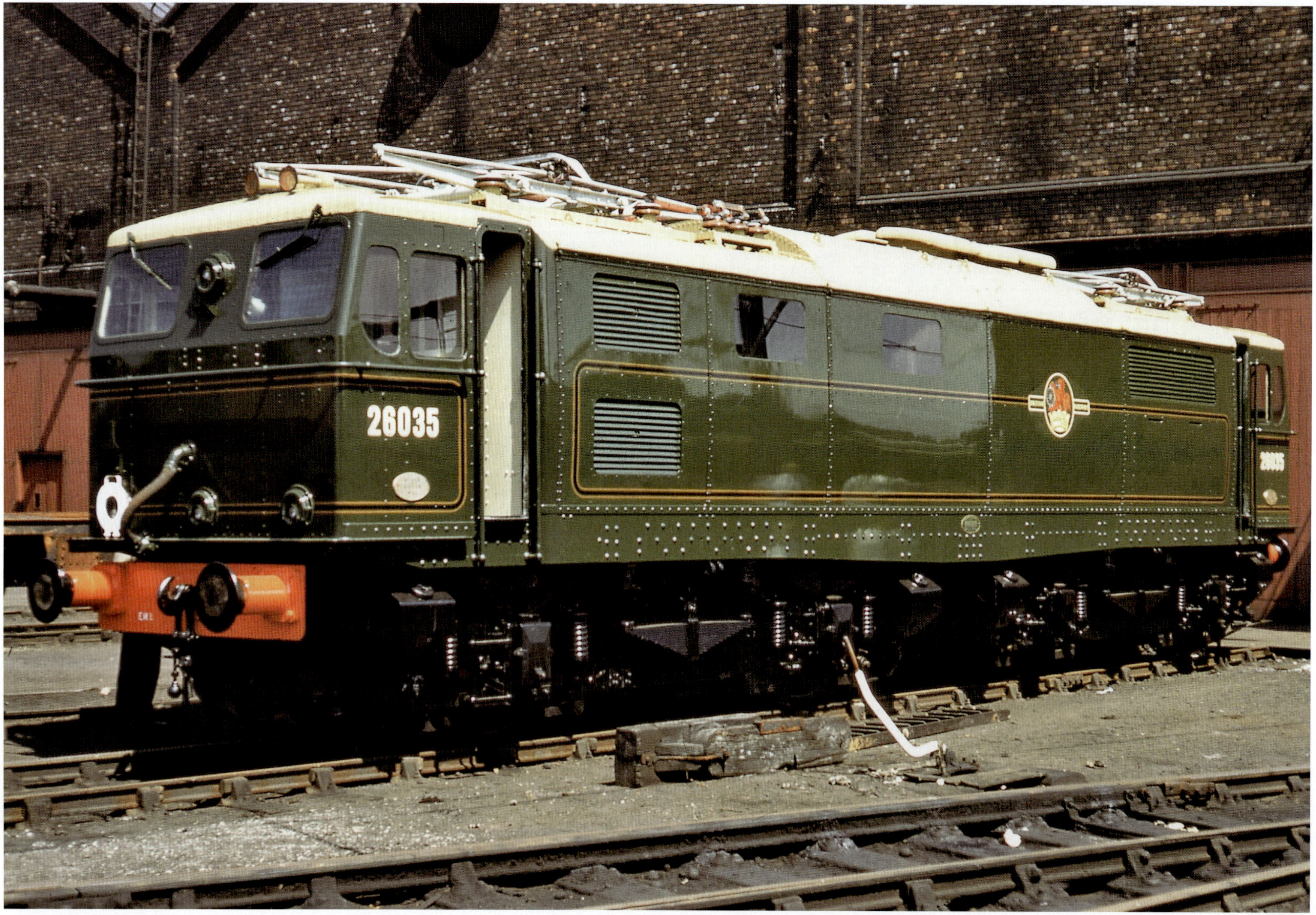
26035
26035

Opposite: Another of the many pre-grouping railway companies' workshops to close completely during the sixties was to be found at Gorton near Manchester, having passed from the Manchester, Sheffield & Lincolnshire Railway into the Great Central Railway before the grouping in 1923 as part of the LNER. They had already constructed the production Woodhead 1,500v dc electric locomotives during the fifties here and they continued to maintain the fleet until the works closed on 31 May 1963. Certainly, the finish on 26035 parked ex-works here on 26 June 1960 looks exemplary. After Gorton had closed the maintenance for the 1,500v dc electrics was shared with Crewe taking the majority and Doncaster helping out with a few as required too. *Colour Rail*

The early history of the ten Type 2 Bo-Bo Baby Deltics from English Electric was certainly troubled to say the least, as a contrast to their other designs. In order to maintain a good working relationship with the British Railways decision makers who would award production contracts for further locomotives, it came as no surprise that a deal was struck to rebuild and refurbish all of what later became Class 23 back at the Vulcan Foundry who built them. On this visit to Doncaster Works in July 1964 we find the recently returned and rebuilt D5909 awaiting testing and acceptance back into service five years after being first delivered here in June 1959. Further problems and being such a small class saw the first withdrawals with four of the class taken out of traffic during 1968, four more the year after leaving just D5905 and D5909 to survive into early 1971, by which time D5909 would be the only one to be painted into blue livery.
Strathwood Library Collection

An interesting line up of heavyweight 1Co-Co1 designs in the yard of Derby Works greets us on 23 April 1961, with D292, 10203 and D25 all in a line. The eight-year working life of 10203 would end the following year, when it was put into open storage here after October 1962 as a prelude to being withdrawn on 7 December 1963. Another heavyweight prototype design would instead be loaned to British Rail from January 1968 until March 1971 by Hawker Siddeley with their HS4000 Co-Co design capable of 125mph, or so they said, and packing a 4,000hp power rating. The downside was found within these original bogies as delivered here at Crewe Works to distribute its massive 133-ton weight. The solution agreed with the powers to be within Crewe Works hierarchy was to change the bogies to those used on Class 47s for the remainder of its trials in Britain.
Photos: Strathwood Library Collection & Michael Morant Collection

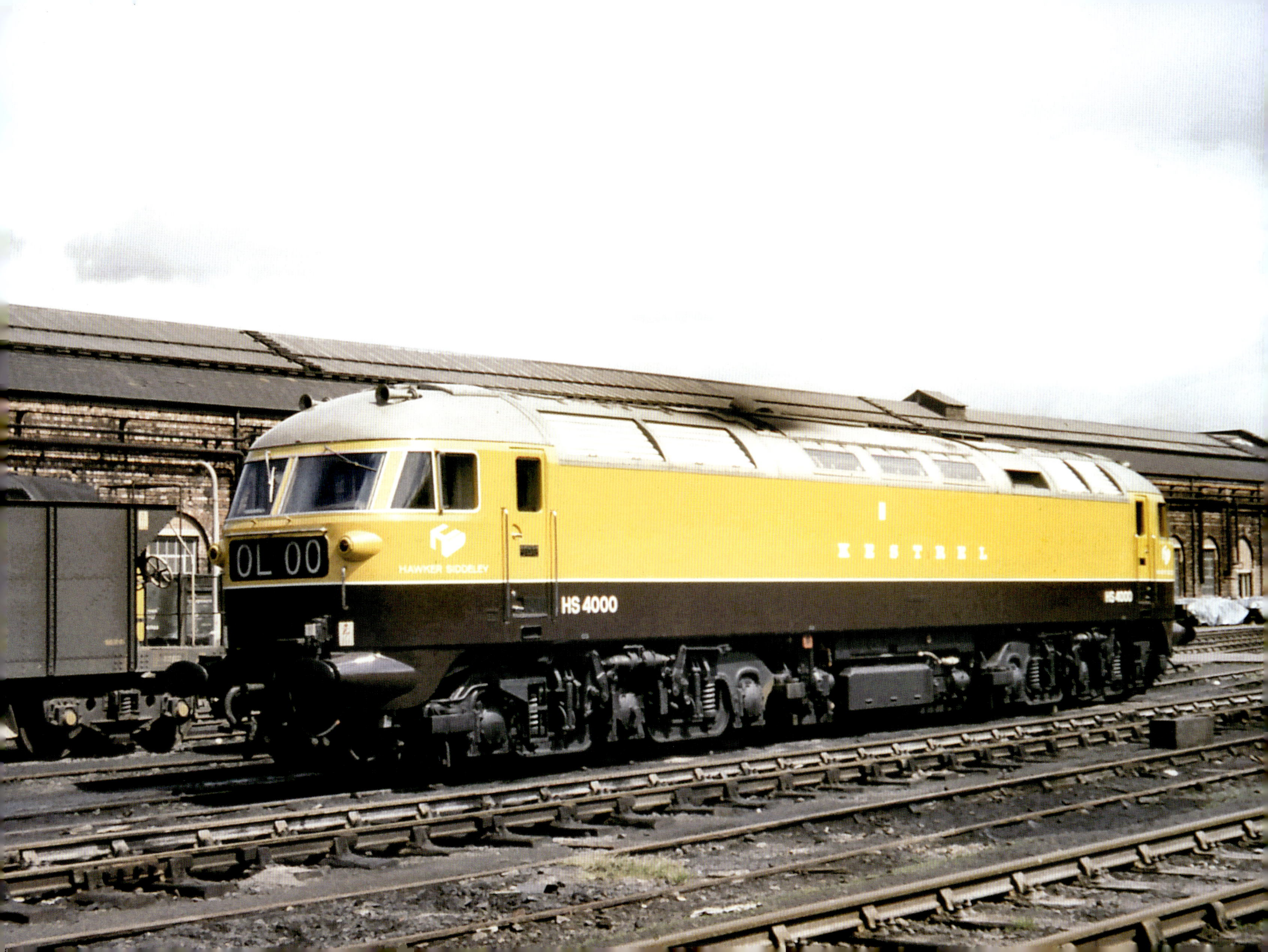
OL 00
HAWKER SIDDELEY
KESTREL
HS 4000
HS 4000

The headcode and brake dust collected upon its bogies and flanks suggests D440 has already been out on test in this visit to Crewe Works in September 1968, as another new Class 50 delivery from English Electric's Vulcan Foundry stands behind also awaiting acceptance. *Dave Langham Collection*